Alcoholism in the African Family

A CHRISTIAN PERSPECTIVE

Hilliard K. Dela Dogbe

WOELI PUBLISHING SERVICES
ACCRA
2011

Published by
Woeli Publishing Services
P.O. Box NT 601
Accra New Town
Ghana
Tel: (233-0302) 229294/227182
E-mail: woelipublishing@yahoo.co.uk
woeli@woelipublishing.com
© Hilliard K. Dela Dogbe 2011
ALL RIGHTS RESERVED
ISBN 978 9988 626 78 5

PRODUCED IN GHANA
Designed and typeset by Woeli Publishing Services, Accra
Printed by Paragon Printing Press, Accra New Town

Contents

Foreword

The publication of *Alcoholism in the African Family* represents a significant stride forward in remedying the paucity of literature on the topic of alcoholism from a distinctly African (specifically Ghanaian) perspective. The author rightfully advocates for a "wholistic" approach to the subject of alcoholism as a total disease. He convincingly articulates the urgency of dealing with addiction as it has ravaged the populace of Ghana, bringing untold suffering and pain to individuals, families, faith communities and the nation as a whole. As a native Ghanaian, the author writes "from the inside out!" That is to say that his social location lends credence to the authenticity of what he writes as an indigenous person. He creatively introduces the reader to the pulse and fabric of life in his African context.

Writing from the perspective of the Christian tradition, he does a thorough job of tracing the etymology of the biblical witness as it relates to the use of alcohol, as well as delineating the ecclesiatical disposition of various Christian churches and their attitudes and concomitant policies with regard to alcohol use. In so doing, he introduces the reader to the "worldview" of Ghanaians that by definition is religious and spiritual in nature. He makes a cogent case not only for the centrality of the spiritual which is endemic to the African lifestyle, but clearly articulates the unique perspective and power of that religious view as permeating the totality of Ghanaian life.

He does stellar work in introducing the reader to the *cultural mindset* of Ghanaians for whom alcohol plays a significant role in their social and spiritual lives. He fleshes out the tension that develops between ritualistic, social and religious use set in juxtaposition to the deleterious and damaging abuse of alcohol on the individual and the family. He employs the insights of family systems theory as it comes to expression in the Ghanaian context, to delineate the dynamics of interaction in a family where addiction prevails. The parallel process that operates between the one who is "afflicted" with the addiction and those who are adversely "affected" (significant others in the social matrix), creates disease for all concerned as significant others "enable" the addictive process and often develop themselves the phenomenon of codependency.

The etiology concerning the conspiracy of silence around this illness is attributed to the power of disgrace and shame. Dogbe carefully elucidates the manner in which this phenomenon factors into the process of addiction and exacerbates an already challenging situation. Until such time that attitudes are altered and addiction is seen as a medical problem as opposed to a moral problem, the public and personal denial of the reality and power of addiction will remain intact. It becomes readily apparent that it is only in dealing constructively with the stigma of disgrace shame that renders alcoholism as an unsanctioned illness, that admission of the existence of addiction in the family can be successfully and effectively addressed.

Methodologically, the author employs a qualitative approach to his research. He collects his raw data via a fourfold process of interviews in order to ascertain the views, ideas and feelings about alcohol use and addiction specifically among the Ewe people of southeastern Ghana. The four categories of people interviewed are:

1. Individuals randomly selected from within the Ewe community.
2. Personal interviews with individuals struggling with addiction to alcohol.
3. Family members adversely affected by the alcohol use.
4. A group or familial interview with several persons (including the addict).

Given the fact that addiction is a stigmatized illness fraught with so much disgrace and shame, the research provides a rare glimpse into the realities experienced by those afflicted and affected by alcoholism. The author is to be commended for his skill in engendering enough trust to provide the reader with such a heretofore unavailable picture of alcoholism among indigenous people. Dogbe makes a cogent argument from his theological perspective for the transformation of the lives of those afflicted with and affected by alcoholism with all of the concomitant exigencies experienced; to a new life of recovery characterized by "shalom." Shalom is the rich Hebrew word that encompasses the totality of that which is good, gracious and life producing. Furthermore, he advocates for the utilization of both indigenous religious rites and rituals set in tandem with the transformative power of God proclaimed in the Christian tradition, as resources for recovery from alcoholism. He seeks to ameliorate the tension between indigenous religious traditions and the Christian tradition. Historically, these two phenomena were cast as polar opposites necessitating relinquishment of the culture and spirituality endemic to the Ewe people in favour of western religious thought. The author argues for the utilization of both for the sake of healing and health for the people of Ghana from the impact of alcoholism.

While reading this volume, three words came to mind that characterize this remarkable work. It is *"comprehensive"* in nature as the author explores so many aspects and facets of this phenomenon known as addiction to alcohol. Secondly, it is *"integrative"* in blending insights garnered from the northern hemisphere of research and then contrasted and coupled with in-depth insights from the southern hemisphere. The book also promulgates the use of religion *and* science that have also been portrayed as being antithetical to one another. Thirdly, the book takes seriously the matter of *"indigenization,"* that is, it focuses on the specificity of context and culture as these relate to the human condition created by the phenomenon of alcoholism or addiction. As readers, you will be amazed at the wealth of information, the depth of insight and the creative imagination of the author as he blesses his reader with truths that will inform, enhance and make effective a ministry of caring among those who are afflicted with and affected by alcoholism in the Ghanaian context. I look forward to the continued research and writing that Hilliard Dogbe will do in the future to further enlighten his readers with knowledge, understanding and wisdom in providing an effective ministry of healing and wholeness for the people of Ghana and by association, for the whole African continent.

ROBERT H. ALBERS
Distinguished Visiting Professor of Pastoral Theology
United Theological Seminary of the Twin Cities
New Brighton, Minnesota, USA

Acknowledgement

"To God be the glory, great things He hath done." God's all-encompassing love and overshadowing grace within a network of family and friends have brought me this far in my journey of life and ministry. I am indeed grateful to God for giving me the strength to undertake this study in spite of my inadequacies and challenges.

I am also grateful to the numerous men and women who surround me with their compassionate presence and for their prayers that sustained me. I am not able to list all of them here. I, however, wish to acknowledge that through the many vicissitudes of life and for many years, their prayers and presence have strengthened me and my family to endure and overcome the throes of addiction.

I am indebted to Rev. Dr. Godfred Ngorli Kodzo Zormelo and Rev. Dr. Kermit J. Degraffenreidt, two fine christian ministers whose insight and practical wisdom were used by God to call me into ministry and for mentoring, guiding and urging me on in this journey of ministeral and academic excellence. To Bishop and Mrs. Kenneth Monroe and the leadership of the A.M.E. Zion Church, I am indeed grateful for the support in my studies and for my ministry.

I am grateful to three teachers without whom this book would neither have been contemplated nor completed. My friend and brother, Rev. Dr. Cyril Fayose of Trinity Theological Seminary, Prof. G. K. Nukunya of the University of Ghana, Legon, and Prof. Bob Albers of the United Seminary of the Twin Cities, are highly appreciated for their encouragement and support, criticisms and guidance throughout this study and for the encouragement to have it published. They painstakingly worked with me through it all, challenged my thoughts and perspectives and stimulated my thinking and creativity with detailed comments, all of which I have found very insightful and helpful. I am also grateful to Bishop Joseph Kow Ghunney, formerly of Trinity Theological Seminary, Accra for arousing my interest in the study of addictive behaviours, and to Prof Deborah van Deusen Hunsinger of Princeton Theological Seminary for helping me deal with my family of origin issues through my classes with her and offering me helpful insights into counselling and psychotherapy. I am indebted to Dr Theresa Latini, Assistant Professor of Pastoral Care and Counselling, Luther Seminary for her encouragement. I wish also to thank the faculty of Trinity Theological Seminary, Ghana for their support.

I acknowledge Rev. David Zungbey, Edina Fiawoo, Phidelia Korbli, Dela Amenuku, Isaac Agyarko, Miranda Zapor, Newlands Hiamey, Teacher Kwame Dogbe, and all those who have in various ways assisted me in this research. I also wish to extend my appreciation to Woeli Atsu Dekutsey of Woeli Publishing Services and his staff, particulary Felicia Asobayireh, for the clarity, skill, attentiveness to detail and the profound respect.

This note of acknowledgement will not be complete without mentioning the overwhelming love and support of my family. My journey through life has been strengthened by the pillar of support from my parents, Rev. Emile Doe Dogbe-Gakpetor and Mrs. Catherine Efuah Dogbe, who have moulded me and have always been there for me. To my sisters, Nelly, Odelia, Ophelia, and Melba, and also to Sena, words are just not enough to express my appreciation for all the encouragement and support you gave me. You have always been there for me and stood with me through the storms. Your love, care and constant words of encouragement and critique have helped to bring me this far. To the entire Dogbe-Gapketor family and to my church family, I say thank you. I am also indebted to the Davies Family, my extended family in the United States for their care and support.

Finally, but most significantly, the long days and nights of toil and sweat could not have been possible without the love, support and graciousness of my wife, Cynthia. She has been the wind beneath my sails. I am indebted to her for her taking charge of the home all the time that I had to be away on this project. I am also very grateful for the love and patience of my beloved babies, Delali and Delasi, who constantly made me smile in the midst of my stress and who have patiently tolerated my long absences from home.

To my family and to the youth of today and all families in the throes of alcohol addiction, I dedicate this book.

1

Alcohol Use in Ghana

Introduction

Alcohol is by far the most widely used drug[1] among both adults and young people in Ghana. Its widespread acceptance, use and abuse have deep historical roots.[2] The social acceptability of alcohol has tended to erode or disguise its true nature as an addictive drug. Attention to alcohol-related problems continues to be viewed as a major medical, social, and health issue. Hence, the destructive effects of alcohol call for intense concern and study. Alcoholism, the addiction to or uncontrolled dependence on alcohol, is a problem that affects the "whole person" intellectually, physically, emotionally, socially, and spiritually. Popular Ghanaian folktales usually reflect the social nature and use of alcohol, thus affirming its commonality in Ghana.

Alcoholism is generally characterized as a family disease in the sense that its socio-economic, spiritual, physical, psychological and emotional effects on the family are enormous and devastating. Families and homes of alcoholics suffer levels of degradation and stigmatization. They are also affected spiritually, physically, emotionally, socially and economically. This, to an extent, may reflect the negative perception held by society about alcoholism and further buttress the fact that alcoholism affects not only the individual but the family as well as the entire community at large. The relational and communal nature of our "Africanness" also

---

[1] A drug is any chemical substance which when taken into the body changes how a person thinks and feels by altering one's mood. It produces physical, mental, emotional, behavioural, or spiritual change in the user. Cocaine, heroine, marijuana, etc., are examples of other drugs or mood altering substances.

[2] See Emmanuel Akyeampong. *Drink, Power, and Social Change: A Social History of Alcohol in Ghana, c. 1800 to Recent Times.* Portsmouth, NH: Heinemann, 1996.

emphasizes, as in family systems theory, the fact that whatever affects the individual member of the family affects the whole family as well as the community.

Whether alcoholism is viewed as an illness from the medical, spiritual or psychosocial point of view or as a combination of all of the aforementioned, it is agreed by all that alcoholism or alcohol addiction is undesirable, an infraction and undesired departure from what is considered normal or acceptable. It is to this end that a quest for wholeness or health for the alcoholic must be total and complete, encompassing the entire family, so as to avoid its destructive progression and ensnaring effects on the family.

Wholeness is an indispensable constituent or feature of the embodiment of the human personality, the realization of which everyone strives to achieve for survival. All of humankind lives in a physical and emotional environment which ultimately influences one's functioning, and defines one's belief system vis à vis one's pattern of behaviour. According to systemic thinking, wholeness means the essential components of the individual connecting and interacting so as to maintain a dynamic balance. This invariably cannot be attained outside the context of one's environment. Thus, one's worldview is ultimately shaped and defined by the cultural influences to which one has been exposed. This is to say, one's worldview which invariably reflects one's cultural exigency, is what basically informs one's view of alcoholism, generally defines one's concept of wholeness and therefore informs, influences, stimulates or propels one accordingly.

Consequently, Gaba surmises that, for the Ewes of southeastern Ghana, their religious life is what defines their worldview. To be able to accordingly reflect on the way of life of the Ewe people is to reflect on their spiritual and religious worldview. Anything outside this context will only tend to be partial and not reflective of the people. It is, however, important to note that akin with most traditional African cultures, the thought and health systems of the Ewes are organized in ways which do not relegate the quest for wholeness or healing to the sole realm of the spiritual or the physical only. Solutions to whatever problem or illness are sought within the framework of religion and community. Thus, the sacred and the secular are not considered in isolation of each other but as an integral part of one's worldview.

Due to the pervasive and insidious nature of alcoholism and its destructive effects on the family at large, one is therefore tempted to ask: Is alcoholism really a problem? Is it possible for the alcoholic and his/her family to attain a total balance in life through a meaningful relationship with God and community?

This work attempts to investigate what happens among the Ewes of southeastern Ghana; their view on alcoholism and its healing processes. In systemic thinking, it has been established that problems are located in "the structure of the system rather than in the nature of the symptomatic member."[3] This implies that the cause of the problem of any individual could lie in the relational patterns that exist among family members. Symptoms of such problems may surface in many forms in the individual and in many ways including alcoholism. Thus, any healing process must consider the whole family as part of the process and not just treating the individual patient. This study will therefore look out for such patterns among the Ewes of south-eastern Ghana.

Consequently, what does the alcohol problem mean for the Church in Africa? What are the peculiar challenges that threaten the life of the alcoholic and his/her family in a quest for wholeness in this African Christian milieu? What is the role of pastoral theologians in the pursuit of wholeness for the alcoholic? Where is the place of the family in this process? These and several other questions arise as one considers alcoholism in the family among the Ewes of southeastern Ghana in relation to the issue of health and wholeness.

Extent of the Problem

The Ghana Medical Association (GMA) noted that, in one year, about 5 million Ghanaians consumed over 36 million litres of *Akpeteshie* (illicit gin), as well as 1 million litres of gin, about 15 million cartons of beer, and also an unquantifiable quantity of

---

[3] Edwin H. Friedman. *Generation to Generation: Family Process in Church and Synagogue*. New York: The Guilford Press, 1985, p. 19.

palm wine and *pito*.[4] This demonstrates the increasing consumption of alcohol, and by extension, the increasing problem that increased consumption inflicts on the Ghanaian society as a whole.

A World Health Organization's (WHO's) Global Status Report on Alcohol 2004 stated that "deaths from an overdose of alcohol are probably more frequent in most societies than deaths from illicit drug overdoses . . . Outbreaks of poisoning deaths from contaminants in alcoholic beverages are also a regular feature of some developing societies."[5] Studies show that 7.3% of males the world over are alcoholics while 1.3% of women suffer from the same problem. A rather large 4.3% of adults above age 20 are alcohol dependent and an immeasurable number are alcohol abusers.[6]

The reality of this problem in Ghana is such that it affects the resources of mental health institutions, law enforcement agencies and families. Statistics available from the Accra Psychiatric Hospital shows that out of a total of 3,370 admissions in 2002, 18.6% or 670 represent alcoholism and substance abuse, of which 174 or 4.6% were for alcoholism only. By 2003, alcoholics alone increased to 6.6% or 220 of a total of 3,295. In 2004 and 2005, the percentage of alcoholics was 5% of total admissions of 3,753 and 3,597 respectively. Though there has been a little drop in the figures, this is not to suggest a lessening number of alcoholics in this society. These figures are not reflective of the whole country (Ghana) since they are figures from the Accra Psychiatric Hospital alone. It was also noted that though alcoholism is on the ascendancy, unlike other drug abuse, cases of alcoholism are not viewed as a mental or physical illness and therefore not reported. The "conspiracy of silence" through denial also tends to make family members cover it up.

Alcoholism has severe effects: physical, social, emotional, economical, spiritual and psychological, on both the individual

---

[4] www.ghanaweb.com. A Ghana News Agency (GNA) Report. 15 December, 2003. *Akpeteshie* is a locally distilled gin. *Pito* is also a locally brewed porridge-like beer made from millet.

[5] Frank Kwadwo Boateng. "Alcohol Consumption Alarming," in *Daily Graphic*, 16 May, 2007 p. 9.

[6] www.alcoholics.com. 2007.

and the family. Thus, for each alcoholic identified, there are several other individuals (family members) who suffer either directly or indirectly as a result. With the increasing incidence of alcoholism, we are then confronted with an ever widening circle of dysfunctional individuals and families. This suggests that the problem of alcoholism cannot be ignored by the church or pastors since its effects are far-reaching, going beyond the individual alcoholic and his family, permeating the church as well as having a consequential effect on its parishioners. It is a problem that affects "the whole person," and recovery from its comprehensive damage takes hard work, retraining, and time. Though occasionally, an alcoholic may miraculously be "delivered" from his or her physical craving for alcohol, "there is no instant cure for the spiritual and psychological damage inflicted by chemical addiction."[7]

Current models of rehabilitation seem to focus on the individual alcoholic with little or nothing done to cater to the affected family. To a large extent, the alcoholic undergoes therapy in isolation from his or her family. Little wonder that most rehabilitated alcoholics are unable to reintegrate with their families after rehabilitation and often relapse due to the inability of the family to maintain homeostasis.[8]

It has been suggested that alcohol does not only affect the whole family but rather it involves the whole family. Despite the devastating effects of alcohol in the Ghanaian milieu, no research has been made to consider its effects on the family and the consequent restoration of the family into wholeness. Moreover, most treatment programmes tend to focus on the individual alcoholic while the family is used just as an aid "to get the addict better." This, according to Lillian Hyatt, is a problem that calls for immediate attention so as to make healing and restoration effective.[9]

Whereas literature is replete with works on alcoholism, its

---

[7] Anderson Spickard and Barbara R. Thompson. *Dying for a Drink: What You Should Know About Alcoholism.* Dallas: Word Publishers, 1985 p. 15.

[8] The term, homeostasis has to do with a balanced steady state of equilibrium.

[9] Lillian Hyatt. "Confronting the System's Denial: Are We Really Reaching the Whole Family?" in *The Awakening: A Substance Abuse Therapeutic Program: Treatment Manual,* August 1992. p. 17f.

effects on the individual alcoholic and the family, how to effect recovery, etc., within western culture, there is sparse work on alcoholism in the family and how wholeness may be secured for both the individual alcoholic and his/her family together within the African context. As one reflects on the systemic theory in relation to addiction, one is persuaded to ask: What are the effects of alcoholism on the individual and the family? How are families of alcoholics — *parents, wives, husbands, and children* — confronting their own broken lives and seeking healing for their deepest wounds? What are the implications for pastoral counselling within the African setting, particularly in the face of the growing incidence of alcoholism and its attendant problems in the family? As one reflects on these questions, one is confronted with the fact that alcoholism is a complex illness. "While the *alcoholic* counts on the family to enable his/her own *alcohol use*, the family members count on the *alcoholic* to enable their own *unhealthy way of living*" (Italics mine)[10] It is imperative that in seeking restoration of the individual, a holistic approach be employed, one that seeks to unravel and understand subtle but significant interrelation between the illness, the alcoholic, the dynamic of his/her family setting and subsequent health of all parties involved. The system is therefore very important and entrée into it is not with the identified patient or individual afflicted, but those who are adversely affected. It has been suggested that significant others become more ill than the one who is afflicted. Thus, Albers asserts that "while much emphasis has been placed on the person who is afflicted, caregivers dare never forget those who are adversely affected."[11]

It is important to note that implied in the term "wholistic" (please note the word, "wholistic" spelt with a "w" is being used advisedly) or wholeness in this study is not only the totality of the individual alcoholic who is suffering but the totality of the system, of which the individual is a part. The current study, while seeking to suggest constructive but "wholistic" ways of restoring the system or family to health and wholeness, primarily

---

[10] *The Awakening. A Substance Abuse Therapeutic Program: Treatment Manual* (August, 1992) Week 6, p. 1.

[11] Robert H. Albers. "Continuity and Change in the Continuum of Care." *Journal of Ministry in Addiction and Recovery*, Vol. 5(2) 1998 p. 4.

attempts to answer the questions: What are the effects of alcoholism on the individual and his/her family among the Ewes? How do we restore alcoholics and their families to wholeness? What traditional therapies are available for treating alcoholics and their families?

It is my contention that alcoholism is a reality among the Ewes of southeastern Ghana aside from the stigmatization that the individual alcoholic experiences.

Significance of the Study

The family is a very important unit in the African cultural milieu and anything that affects the stability of the family is of much interest to the good people of Ghana. The study will provide knowledge about the dangers inherent in alcohol use and abuse. It will also aid families to confront their own broken lives as they seek healing for restoring the family to homeostasis or balance. All the treatment facilities interrogated in this research have no treatment plan for families aside from using them as support for the individual alcoholic. Thus, treatment facilities, psychologists, social workers and other care-givers, including pastors and pastoral counsellors will also find this study very useful. It will help them gain a better insight into this insidious problem, its nature, cause and scope so as to better develop a more comprehensive approach to helping alcoholics and their families. Other areas of significance that will find this work useful are government agencies, policy-makers; for academia it will provide an impetus for further research. Most researchers have contended that a focus on spirituality is the most successful way to restore the alcoholic. Spirituality must be culture-specific and as such these western strategies will not be useful in considering treatment plans for the African Christian context. This work is therefore very significant for the church as she attempts to redirect parishioners towards the Ultimate Deity and thus wholeness.

Literature on Alcoholism in the Family

In *Understanding and Counselling Persons with Alcohol, Drug and Behavioural Addictions*, Howard Clinebell notes that alcoholism is increasingly destroying families and it is becoming rare not to find a person or family whose life is not impacted directly or indirectly by alcohol and drug problems.[12] In line with the WHO and the American Medical Association, Clinebell posits that alcoholism or alcohol addiction is an illness characterized by the craving for and continuing excessive use of alcoholic beverages in ways that are harmful to the users and many others. There is, however, a diminishing freedom to interrupt the pattern by conscious action or intention. Thus, if it continues unrecognized and untreated, due to its nature as a progressive, chronic and potentially fatal disease, excessive alcohol use and abuse could result in severe physiological and psychiatric problems.

Clinebell suggests that issues relating to alcoholism must not be generalized due to its baffling variety. Some alcoholics become addicted after extended periods of controlled or social drinking, often at a time of personal crisis. Many, however, become pathological drinkers from a relatively adequate psychological adjustment. About an equal number have other drinking patterns that suggest they quite obviously were disturbed persons before their addiction.

To avoid the dangers of generalization, Clinebell lists two types of alcoholics: the *low-bottom* and *high-bottom* alcoholics. Low-bottom alcoholics refer to those who have reached a low point of personal and social disintegration and this represents less than one out of ten alcoholics. The majority of alcoholics are still able to hold their jobs and live with their families, but are less adequate or functional as parents and spouses, as well as being less efficient in their work. They are often depressed, tired and generally run-down. Alcoholics at such a level of minimal social disintegration are called high-bottom alcoholics. Even though alcohol is giving such people problems, they are "dragging their anchors," because alcohol has not sent them off from normal social integration. Steady alcoholics comprise those who drink almost everyday. By contrast is the periodic alcoholic which refers to one who is abstinent for periods ranging from a few days to several months.[13] It is, however, very common for one to move from one typology

---

[12] Howard Clinebell. *Understanding and Counselling Persons with Alcohol, Drug, and Behavioural Addictions.* Revised and enlarged edition. Nashville: Abingdon Press, 1998 p. 21.

[13] Clinebell, *Understanding and Counselling,* p. 33ff.

to the other in the development of one's alcoholism due to its progressive nature.[14]

Clinebell contends that "alcohol is associated with more human tragedies and costs than all other drugs combined."[15] It has further been observed in a recent study by Don Powell that of the ten leading causes of death, alcohol is a contributing factor in six of them. Also, about one third of all families are affected, directly or indirectly, by some form of alcohol problem.[16] Thus, in addition to the millions of alcoholics and problem drinkers, there are also several million family members devastated by the illness. Although there are several measurable costs of alcohol abuse and addiction, more often than not, its devastating effects on the family are immeasurable, non-quantifiable and intangible due to its disproportional occurrence coupled with the fact that there are many cases of alcoholism that are not known.

Clinebell asserts that alcoholism is a family disease in the sense that its devastating effects are not limited to the individual but encompasses the whole family and community at large. Thus, the most efficient and effective way of enabling movement towards recovery of the family is to work with the whole family-friend network.

> First, as in all intimate social systems, the emotional and relational climate of the whole system influences all those in it. Second, anything that disturbs, diminishes, or enhances any member's well being inevitably impacts everyone else's degree of wellness. And third, a plethora of socio-psychological studies have shown that mates and children of severally addicted people often are nearly as disturbed, anxious, and in need of help as are the addicted. The whole family needs guidance and help, not only for recovery for their acute crisis, but also for the growth that needs to follow.[17]

---

[14] See E.M. Jellinek. *The Disease Concept of Alcoholism*. New Haven: Hillhouse Press, 1960; and Robert V. Seliger, *How to Help an Alcoholic. A Brief Medical Summarization with Practical Suggestions and Tests*. Columbus, Ohio: School and College Service, 1951.

[15] Clinebell, *Understanding and Counselling*, p. 46.

[16] Clinebell, *Understanding and Counselling*, p. 46

[17] Clinebell, *Understanding and Counselling*, p. 398.

Recognizing the impoverishing and enormous psychological and physiological damage on families, "it is high time that caring people in all religious traditions responded to help enable this immense, wasted, God-given potential to be used for the well-being of not only addicted people, but also the whole human family."[18]

In some sense, the crises of alcoholism are considered as social deviations that often do not elicit community support for family members. Thus, the crisis of alcoholism is said to be more difficult for families than the trauma of grief because addictions are "unstructured and stigmatized crises."[19] Consequently, families often respond with feelings of humiliation, alienation, self-isolation, and baffled confusion. Clinebell thereby contends that applying family systems theory to addictions and recovery is a very necessary therapeutic procedure that considers the family as an operational system with an identity and family personality that is more than the sum of its individual members. Thus, every family member is profoundly influenced by the health or sickness of that organic social system. Healthy or unhealthy changes in any one member therefore impact the entire system and every member of the system.[20]

Clinebell's position on alcoholism in the family generally agrees with the position of this study. Though he does not engage very well, the general differences in family dynamics and how the individual's alcoholism affects different systems differently, he affirms spiritual causes of alcoholism as a very powerful component. This, to a very large extent, is very significant as one considers the thesis of this chapter. According to Clinebell, a very significant cluster of causes that are often ignored but crucial to addiction and recovery "are the powerful and often-hidden spiritual, religious, and ethical disturbances" — the existential vacuums — that often play crucial roles in the addictive process."[21] True to these spiritual causes is the fact that alcoholics and their families need to be helped in satisfying their spiritual hunger.

---

[18] Clinebell, *Understanding and Counselling*, p. 48.
[19] Clinebell, *Understanding and Counselling*, p. 400.
[20] Clinebell, *Understanding and Counselling*, p. 400f.
[21] Clinebell, *Understanding and Counselling*, p. 89.

In *Family Therapy in the Treatment of Alcoholism,* Edward Kaufman notes the existence of an intimate relationship between the problem of alcoholism and family systems. For Kaufman, this relationship may be singular, as in the case of social individual alcoholism in a stable and healthy family system, or it may be quite generalized, involving several generations or groups of kin.[22] Kaufman presents four descriptive types of family systems of alcoholism that are not necessarily definitive, but are, however, illustrative of a broad spectrum of family involvements in alcoholism. Intervention moves must therefore be utilized to reflect the different types of systems. These four family systems in which alcoholism is a major problem are first, the *functional family system.* This is a family with an alcoholic member and in this system, there is stability and parents maintain a loving relationship. "Drinking in the alcoholic partner(s) does not evolve as a result of family stress, but primarily from response to social strains and/or personal neurotic conflict."[23] This system usually occurs in the early phases of the disease and could deteriorate as alcoholism progresses.

The second is the *neurotic enmeshed family system* or what can be described as the alcoholic family. Here, alcoholic behaviour interrupts normal family tasks, causes conflicts, shifts roles, and demands that family members adapt in response. Drinking triggers anger in the drinker and also creates physical dysfunction which in turn produces marital conflicts. In such a system, anxiety is high and causes everyone to do more of what they are already doing. Accordingly, drinking to relieve anxiety, and family anxiety in response to drinking, can spiral into a crisis. In this system, everyone feels guilty and responsible for each other, particularly for the alcoholic and his or her drinking. This is because stresses in any single family member immediately affect the entire family. Communication is often not direct but through a third party. Likewise, conflicts are triangulated (projected) onto another family member. In such a situation, as non-alcoholic members take over management of the family, the alcoholic is relegated

---

[22] Edward Kaufman. "Family Therapy in the Treatment of Alcoholism" in *Alcoholism and Substance Abuse: Strategies for Clinical Intervention,* Thomas Bratter and Gary Forrest, eds. New York: The Free Press, 1985 p. 377.

[23] Kaufman, *Family Therapy,* p. 377.

12   *Alcoholism in the African Family: A Christian Perspective*

to a child's status, which perpetuates drinking.[24]

The *disintegrated family system* is the system where the alcoholic is temporarily separated from the alcoholic family and is often in a later state of the neurotic enmeshed system, although the functional system may also regress directly to a disintegrated system. The fourth system, the *absent family system* is where the alcoholic is permanently separated from the family. In this system, the alcoholic has little or no family contact and few social or vocational relationships.[25] For Kaufman, "the structures, attitudes and function of the family system have been shown to be a crucial variable in the successful outcome of alcoholism treatment."[26] He further posits that to have a much broader view of alcoholism as a family problem one would have to look beyond marital partners to considering the entire family system, including the families of origin, the lifestyle of children from alcoholic families, and the kin structures of the extended family system.

Duncan Stanton, in *The Family and Drug Abuse: Concepts and Rationale,* affirms that families differ in their composition and each family must be considered in its uniqueness without generalizations.[27] Also, "viewing the individual apart from his or her family can give only an incomplete picture of the person's daily functioning."[28] For Stanton, it is therefore necessary to find clear ways to strengthen the resistances and minimize the exaggerations since "the family is a force that helps resist or exaggerate the stress of other environmental factors."[29] This is very significant as the family attempts to maintain its equilibrium. It is worth noting that causes and effects on the family are not only physical or psycho-social. The spiritual dimension to causes and healing of alcoholism cannot be relegated to an insignificant role. This is considered in the following reviews:

---

[24] Kaufman, *Family Therapy,* p. 378
[25] Kaufman, *Family Therapy,* p. 379
[26] Kaufman, *Family Therapy,* p. 382.
[27] M. Duncan Stanton. "The Family and Drug Abuse: Concepts and Rationale" in *Alcoholism and Substance Abuse: Strategies for Clinical Intervention,* ed. Thomas Bratter and Gary Forrest. New York: The Free Press, 1985 pp. 398-429.
[28] Stanton, *The Family and Drug Abuse,* p. 398.
[29] Stanton, *The Family and Drug Abuse,* p. 425.

Literature on Healing of Alcoholism

According to Clinebell, primary prevention of addiction and full recovery from it often requires people to learn healthy, non-chemical ways to satisfy their inescapable spiritual or existential hunger. There is, therefore, the need for the church and clergy to facilitate this crucial learning for healthy spiritual growth.

> There is no area of human suffering in which healthy religion has given a more convincing demonstration of its healing, growth-nurturing power than in problems of addictions ... Authentic spirituality offers hopeful resources for dealing with addictions.[30]

This assertion was recognized by an internationally known psychiatrist, Carl Gustav Jung in Zurich who is noted to have told an alcoholic that "nothing but a religious conversion could give him any lasting help."[31] Thus, religious approaches can help individuals by uplifting their spirit above daily frustrations, disappointments, drudgery and interpersonal conflicts that contribute to the addictions. A spiritual dimension is therefore an essential part of any effective recovery programme. There is therefore a need to nurture healthy spirituality through a process of transformation.

Keller, Albers and several other writers, just like Clinebell, have acknowledged the afore-mentioned causes of alcoholism, particularly the disease concept; though Clinebell goes further to affirm spiritual and religious causality. They have generally asserted that authentic spirituality is a hopeful resource in dealing with alcoholism. One body at the forefront of restoring the alcoholic to wholeness, is the Alcoholics Anonymous (AA). Of help too is the Twelve-Step programme which is primarily based on spirituality since it is grounded in a loving higher power.[32] Clinebell argues that "in all the long, dark, dismal history of the problem of alcoholism, the brightest ray of hope and help is

---

[30] Clinebell, *Understanding and Counselling*, p. 23.
[31] Clinebell, *Understanding and Counselling*, p. 23.
[32] See *Alcoholics Anonymous* (The Big Book) Third Edition. AA World Services Inc., 1976.

Alcoholics Anonymous."[33] This goes to affirm the effectiveness of AA and other twelve-step programmes.

John Keller in his book, *Ministering to Alcoholics*, suggests that admission of powerlessness and self-honesty are essential elements for recovery. It is, therefore, very important to look for God (a higher power) in a spiritual recovery process. Like Clinebell, Keller also suggests that AA is an essential process in any recovery programme. "One can only effectively find his way up and out to sobriety through a dramatic, intense spiritual experience that involved surrender to God in his powerlessness."[34] Thus, though a seemingly difficult process, alcoholics surrender to this reality in their relationship to God find strength in their weakness.[35] According to Keller,

When there is wholehearted surrender, the whole person, conscious and unconscious, has quit fighting, quit resisting reality, given in, accepted defeat and need for help. The omnipotent ego has gone and with this comes humility.[36]

Through humility and meditation, God's strength is perfected in the weaknesses of the alcoholic. "This is not giving up. This is giving in, accepting the reality of powerlessness, of our creaturehood, of our imperfection."[37] As long as the alcoholic continues to fight this problem, either consciously or unconsciously, he or she continues to drink and experiences severe inner tension when sober. When one quits fighting this reality and surrenders, he or she is able to receive strength and the tension subsides.[38] According to Robert Albers, however, this process of surrender culminates in transformation, which is the key to recovery. Transformation in this sense is not merely change but seeking power from God over one's powerlessness as one moves toward restoration.

---

[33] Clinebell, *Understanding and Counselling*, p. 195.
[34] John E. Keller. *Ministering to Alcoholics*, Revised Edition. Minneapolis: Augsburg Fortress, 1991, p. 35.
[35] See also Harry Tiebout. *The Act of Surrender in the Therapeutic Process*. New York: National Council on Alcoholism, n.d P. 6.
[36] Keller, *Ministering to Alcoholics*, p. 51.
[37] Keller, *Ministering to Alcoholics*, p. 51.
[38] Keller, *Ministering to Alcoholics*, p. 51.

Transformation from a theological perspective is a key conceptual framework within which to understand the recovery process from addiction. It is a gift of grace and is a processive phenomenon incorporating the reality of the past, the actuality of the present and the potentiality of the future.[39]

Albers also identifies addiction as a primary spiritual malady with a concomitant physical, psychological and social implications. He, however, associates recovery with a spiritual awakening that results in physical, psychological and social restoration.[40] Sustained recovery, according to Albers, is insured through participating in a caring community. As one surrenders to God, the higher power, in prayerful and trustful confidence, another significant resource available during these times of stress and strain is the presence of a caring community.[41] This suggests that the individual's surrender and eventual transformation must be done within the context of caring relationships of familial or faith congregational networks for restoration to be total and complete.

It is therefore fundamental to give attention to and reflect theologically on the social milieu in which the addicted person lives, namely those significant others such as family members, who are adversely affected by the addiction. Positing an interactive theory of addiction, Albers suggests that "individuals develop addiction in a social matrix of significant others." However configured, this social constellation "is affected by the addiction which in turn has a bearing on the wider social construct of community, nation and world." Transformation therefore must not only be limited to the individual. Rather, "it is only as we allow the spirit of God to transform not only individuals, but families, communities, nation and the world that progress will be made toward a future" which is purposeful and promising to all.[42]

---

[39] Robert Albers. "Transformation: The Key to Recovery." *Journal of Ministry in Addiction and Recovery*, Vol. 4(1) 1997. The Haworth Press. p. 23.

[40] Albers, *Transformation*, p. 24.

[41] Albers, *Transformation*, p. 33.

[42] Albers, *Transformation*, p. 35f.

Several of these concepts on the causes, nature and dynamics of alcoholism and its effects on the family have been explored further in the theoretical frameworks. Needless to say, though scholarship is available in western literature on alcoholism in the family, literature on Africa by Africans is virtually unavailable. Lartey, Masamba ma Mpolo, Kasonga wa Kasonga, Berinyuu, as well as several other African pastoral theologians suggest that in pastoral theology, the contextual worldview of the individual must be of primary concern and must not be ignored in any given situation.[43] A review of Ghunney's work on African spiritual worldview and its impact on alcohol and other drug use is therefore very significant to this study.[44]

African Literature on Alcoholism

Joseph Ghunney posits that the several theories that have been postulated to explain the causes of alcohol and other drug use, such as genetic transmission, social stress, biosocial, psychosocial, social learning, observational and the disease concept, could be irrelevant in the African context, particularly Ghana. This is because within this context, supernatural powers are believed to influence people's use of alcohol. For Ghunney, the belief in the supernatural is an important aspect of the social structure of Ghanaian culture. Diseases and misfortunes may be assumed to have spiritual and supernatural cause. Without excepting alcohol or drug abuse, Ghunney suggests that any moral deviation of the community's taboos or acts that incur the displeasure of the spirit world is believed to invite calamities and misfortunes. People will therefore generally seek help from a spiritualist to understand the source of their afflictions and healing for their broken lives. Thus alcoholism and other drug use are ascribed to supernatural causes due to this worldview.[45]

---

[43] See Emmanuel Lartey, Daisy Nwachuku and Kasonga Wa Kasonga (eds). *The Church and Healing: Echoes From Africa*. Frankfurt am Main: Peter Lang, 1994; and *The Risks of Growth: Counselling and Pastoral Theology in the African Context*. World Council of Churches, 1985.

[44] Joseph Kow Ghunney. African Spiritual Worldview: Its Impact on Alcohol and Other Drug Use by Senior Secondary School Students in Ghana, a PhD Dissertation. Maryland: Loyola College, 1994.

[45] Ghunney, *African Spiritual Worldview*.

In the above review, the writers have all sought to explain the nature and dynamics of alcoholism and its recovery. Though western scholarship has made inroads into research on alcoholism in the family as it relates to family systems thinking, and also puts emphasis on spirituality as essential to any recovery process, the use of such resources in the African context will be tantamount to putting "square pegs in round holes." This is because such theories do not reflect the African context. According to Lartey, historical events such as globalization have succeeded in transmitting particular values throughout the world. However, it is imperative for "pastoral theologians to undertake an analysis of their own contexts with the realization that personal needs that call for pastoral responses in each context are embedded in the social, economic, cultural, religious and political issues unearthed and explored thereby."[46] Thus taking context seriously means recognizing and affirming that people are different and are confronted by different issues. The fact that contextual analysis involves a search for understanding the worldviews and practices by which people seek to care for themselves makes Ghunney's reflection on African spiritual worldview very relevant.

Nonetheless, even though Ghunney considers very well the pervasive nature of religion and spirituality in African ontology and establishes the communal nature of our "africanness," the work is, however, silent on how the individual's alcoholism or drug use affects families and communities.

This current study seeks to reflect on the nature and dynamics of alcoholism in the African family. It therefore seeks to build a bridge between western scholarship on alcoholism and family systems on the one hand, and the African contextual worldview on the other by building on the work of the above researchers. Several other literary references will be cited in the conceptual framework as well as contextual worldview to support this claim.

---

[46] Emmanuel Lartey. *Pastoral Theology in an Intercultural World.* Great Britain: Epworth, 2006 p. 70f.

2

Contemporary Views About Alcoholism

Alcohol Addiction

This type of addiction is no different from addiction to other drugs. Addiction is a bio-psycho-social and spiritual disease, a primary physical disease which affects all areas of a drug-dependent person's life. Addiction is acceptably described as:

> A disease which is primary, chronic, hereditary, eventually fatal, and may progress from an early psychological susceptibility into a condition characterized by tolerance changes, psychological dependence and loss of control over a mood altering substance.[47]

This study, however, concentrates on alcohol and not on the larger question of chemical dependency of which alcohol is only one manifestation. This is because alcohol, by far, is historically and currently widely and pervasively used in this society. As a "legal drug," its social and personal effects have become a subject of intense concern, study, and activity.[48] However, the problem of alcoholism is still baffling to many. According to Clinebell, few problems have been as inexplicable in nature as alcohol and drug dependence. "No health problem has been studied more extensively than alcoholism."[49] This has brought about new understanding, not only from the point of view of the addicted persons but their families as well.

The World Health Organization (WHO) of the United Nations and other medical associations characterize the compulsive-addictive uses of alcohol as an illness. Primarily, according to Clinebell, the behavioural characteristics of this

---

[47] *The Awakening: A Substance Abuse Therapeutic Manual* (n.d.). Phase 1, Week 2. p. 3.

[48] PCUSA . *Alcohol Use and Abuse: Reports and Recommendations by the Presbyterian Church*. USA (Louisville, KY: Office of Health Ministries) p. 9.

[49] Clinebell, *Understanding and Counselling*, p. 23.

illness are "craving for the psycho-physiological effects of alcohol and continuing excessive use of alcoholic beverages in ways that are harmful to the user and many others."[50] There is also a lessening freedom to disrupt the pattern by conscious action or intention and once it continues unrecognized and untreated, alcoholism is then typified as a "progressive, chronic, and potentially fatal disease" which could result in grave physiological and psychiatric complications.[51] Though the Roman philosopher, Seneca, referred to it as a form of insanity, for some, it is a physiological or psychosomatic illness while for others it is a psychological illness, thus suggesting a mental defect. Others still, contend that it is hereditary in nature.[52] However, the 1990 definition by the American Society of Addiction Medicine (ASAM) is more widely acknowledged. It elucidates the basic distinctiveness of alcoholism:

> Alcoholism is a primary, chronic disease with genetic, psychosocial, and environmental factors influencing its development and manifestations. The disease is often progressive and fatal. It is characterized by continuous or periodic impaired control over drinking, preoccupation with the drug alcohol, use of alcohol despite adverse consequences, and distortions in thinking, most notably denial (*ASAM News* March–April, 1990). [53]

This suggests that alcoholism is a disease whose effects are as painful and destructive as any other disease. When a person drinks, it affects the person mentally, emotionally, physically, spiritually and behaviourally. It overwhelms the individual and the whole family is engulfed in its devastating progressions.

It is, however, worth noting that alcohol is not a stimulant but a depressant which sometimes numbs the person, affecting the brain and other parts of the central nervous system. However, many people continually seek solace in "the bottle" as they struggle to alleviate pain, loneliness, insecurity, fear and the sense

---

[50] Clinebell, *Understanding and Counselling*, p. 25.
[51] Clinebell, *Understanding and Counselling*, p. 25. For more on alcohol as a disease, see E.M. Jellinek, *The Disease Concept of Alcoholism*. New Haven, CT: Yale University Press, 1966.
[52] www.alcoholics.com c 2007.
[53] *The Awakening*: Week 3, p. 9.

of not belonging; some of them compulsively and with a regularity that is injurious and deleterious to them physiologically, psychologically, economically and spiritually. It is in the light of this that alcoholism can be defined. However, not everyone who uses alcohol in excess is diagnosed as an alcoholic, because he/she can still exercise the power of choice.

Alcohol Addiction *vs.* Alcohol Abuse

It is worth noting the subtle difference between alcoholism or alcohol addiction and alcohol abuse. There are those who tend to use alcohol less often and with greater control but with many of the same side effects. These are generally referred to as abusers or problem drinkers. Some also ordinarily refer to such persons as social drinkers. William Kraft refers to such abusers as *normal* or *functional* alcoholics and contends that though they portray similar trends as addicts, the abuser functions relatively well and exercises greater degree of control.[54] This suggests that alcohol abusers will choose when to drink, how much to drink or even if to drink. Though one drinks heavily, one does not have any problem with exercising control.

For the alcohol addict, however, the problem does not end. According to Spickard and Thompson, the alcoholic cannot envisage when he will drink or how much to drink. Even though alcohol may cause the alcoholic some trouble in one or more areas of his/her life such as *family, friends, health, job, finances, legal matters, etc.,* the alcoholic nevertheless continues to drink. Thus, unlike the alcohol abuser, the alcohol addict no longer has control over his own will but that "his internal center for decision-making and free choice has been captured by alcohol."[55] This suggests that the alcoholic has *lost the power of choice.* Thus, the alcoholic can no longer predict what his or her behaviour will be after the first drink. Along with this loss of choice also goes the "loss of control" relative to behaviour. The alcoholic is therefore unable to decide not to drink. This loss of self-control makes it easy to dismiss alcoholism as a problem that is unique to "weak-willed people." However, to characterize this involuntary loss of self-control as a weakness of the will is

---

[54] William F. Kraft. *The Normal Alcoholic.* New York: Alba House, 1999, p. vii.
[55] Spickard and Thompson. *Dying for a Drink,* p. 39.

erroneous because "strong determination is no defense against addiction."[56] It is very difficult to determine where abuse ends and addiction begins though it is still very easy to cross the line. Generally speaking, abusers or problem drinkers are increasingly dependent on the alcohol but not yet physiologically addicted. For this reason, Clinebell describes abusers as "controlled social users."[57] Nevertheless the possibility of their ultimately becoming physiologically addicted increases with excessive intake. Though it is difficult to distinguish between the problem drinker or alcohol abuser and the addict due to its gradual progression or transition from one condition to the other, people overuse alcohol in ways that produce serious problems for themselves as well as others.[58]

The view we take of alcoholism determines the way "we diagnose, treat, and feel about alcoholism."[59] It is therefore very important for one to clearly and consciously be aware of one's personal views, theories and assumptions towards drinking. Such views could either be helpful or harmful. Accordingly, the way one views alcoholism constitutes the meaning alcoholism holds for him or her and therefore highly influences how one experiences, judges, treats, copes with, feels about, and lives with alcoholics.

Models of Addiction

Over the years, several views or models have been put forth as suggested ways of understanding this problem of alcoholism and other drug addictions. Such models include the *moral model, temperance model, psychological or characterological model, social education model*, and the *disease model*. These models are important since they reflect the ways people think of Alcohol and Other Drug Abuse (AODA). One's perspective as well as that of the family tends to indicate which treatment will be beneficial in the long-term.

Though we have hitherto sought to emphasize the disease model for the purpose of treatment, I am becoming more and more convinced of an all-inclusive approach, *the "wholistic"*

---

[56] Spickard and Thompson. *Dying for a Drink*, p. 39.
[57] Clinebell, *Understanding and Counselling*, p. 87.
[58] Clinebell, *Understanding and Counselling*, p. 87f.
[59] Kraft, *Normal Alcoholic*, p. 22.

model, which I contend, is integrative or embraces the true nature of alcoholism. A cursory look at some major categorical classifications of AODA perspectives in a developmental context will therefore be helpful in promoting the "wholistic" model.

Moral Model

This model, also called the traditional model, is the oldest view of AODA. From the point of view of the Moral Perspective, AODA is seen as an infringement of societal rules by the abuser. Proponents feel it is a punishable crime and holds the individual responsible for his or her choices. The church and many in the religious community take this view and criticize alcohol addiction as a sinful act, hence ostracizing the alcoholic.

Temperance Model

This emphasizes the idea of moderation as an impractical task and as primary to the shortcomings of treatment. Abstinence is therefore asserted as the only alternative. The core assumption here is that the addictive and destructive power of the drug is strong; and that it is the drug itself that is the problem and must be cut out of one's life.

Psychological or Characterological Model

This approach views addiction as rooted in abnormalities of personality or character and that an "addictive personality" exists in such individuals and is inherent with a degree of deficit in personal and psychological boundaries.

Social Education Model

This model represents an integrative approach that views AODA as a learned behaviour stemming from cognitive processes and influences affecting modelling, behaviour and genetics. Emphasis is also placed on human environment as key in shaping AODA behaviours.

Disease Model

This model asserts that alcohol and other drug abuse is a unique, irreversible, and progressive disease. Dr. E. M. Jellinek in his seminal work emphasizes these progressions and contends that while alcoholism and addiction cannot be cured, such conditions can be arrested by abstaining from the substance the individual is addicted to.[60]

Whichever way they are interpreted, these models seem to fall short of addressing the complexities involved with the problem of alcoholism. Spiritual causation factors, especially in Africa, have been affirmed as a very necessary root of alcoholism that cannot be ignored. Considering the aforementioned models in isolation of each other, one realizes that though possible, each on its own does not clearly reflect the holistic nature of the disease as a psycho-social, physical, emotional, ethical, spiritual and environmental problem. The "wholistic" model, which seems to be concomitant with the 1990 definition, thus seeks to suggest that to be able to seek wholeness or healing "wholistically," one must consider an integrative approach which suggests that alcoholism is caused by several integrative factors together; physical, psychological, and spiritual, and its treatment must be considered in that context and within the framework of the family and culture to which one belongs.

Most churches, however, in emphasizing the moral model, tend to "whack the back of the head of the alcoholic with the Bible," criticizing the alcoholic for his/her "shameful" act. This position, often taken by the church, does not really reflect the true nature of alcoholism. *This false categorization raises the theological question as to whether alcoholism is a sin that must be absolved or an illness that must be cured.* In an attempt to answer this question, it is worth considering the biblical position on alcohol as well as the various theological views of alcoholism or uses of alcohol.

ALCOHOLISM AND THEOLOGY

Biblical Views on Alcohol

The biblical perspective on the use and misuse of wine is very relevant for this study. Though alcoholism is not really known in biblical times, the characteristic use, functions and abuse of wine has been mentioned in the scriptures. Some people have

---

[60] http://www.family-drug-intervention.net/addiction_models.html.

certainly suggested that biblical references to wine are contradictory. However, a careful study of biblical texts will help us understand it one way or the other. According to James Patrick Holding, the word' wine appears over 200 times in the King James Version (KJV) of the Bible.[61] In the Old Testament, three key words are used for wine: *yayin, skar* and *tirowsh*.[62]

Yayin

According to Patrick Holding, Strong notes the root of this word as meaning "to effervesce." Clearly, one sees it as referring to alcoholic drinks.[63] Probably since it is a loan word, it has cognates in Indo-European language texts: Greek *oinos*, Latin *vinum*, German *wein*. The word is used 140 times, 12 of these in combination with *aekar* ("wine and strong drink," sometimes "wine and beer"). Its intoxicating properties are mentioned at least twenty times. It is mentioned as a common drink, an element in banquets and as the material used in libation offerings (Ex 29:40 and 30:9).

Wine was forbidden to priests while ministering (Lev 10:9 — there is a hint that Nadab and Abihu in Lev 10:1–7 desecrated the sanctuary in drunkenness). Nazirites also and Samson's mother-to-be were to drink no wine or *aekar* (NIV "fermented drink"; Jud 13:4; Num 6:3).[64] The Israelites "ate no bread and drank no wine" during the forty years in the wilderness (Deut 29:6). Kings were to avoid it so as to govern with a clear head (Prov 31:4–5). Solomon warns against the use of wine because of its final tragic consequences (Prov 23:30–31).

Abundance of wine, however, is taken as a symbol of affluence (Gen 49:11–12; I Chr 12:40; Ezek 27:18). There are places that speak of the lift to the feelings that wine brings (Zech 10:7; II Sam 13:28; Est 1:10; Ps 104:15; Eccl 9:7–10; 10:19; Is 55:1). It may be questioned whether in these verses wine is commended

---

[61] James Patrick Holding. *A Little Whine: Is the Bible Contradictory on Wine and Alcohol?* www.tektonics.org/1p/nowine.html.

[62] This word study is mainly taken from Harris, R. L., Archer, G. L., & Waltke, B.K., *Word Studies:Theological Wordbook of the Old Testament* [electronic ed.]. Chicago: Moody Press 1999, c1980.

[63] Holding, *A Little Whine*.

[64] NIV refers to New International Version and AV used later refers to Authorized Version of the Bible.

because of this lift or if the verses use the freedom from inhibition of incipient drunkenness as a symbol of plenty and blessing (cf. Nathan's reference to David's polygamy as a symbol of God's giving him great riches [II Sam 12:8]). Wine is also used in symbolic ways of the drink that wisdom mingles (Prov. 9:2), of the Lord's wrath (Jer 25:15, etc.), of disaster (Ps 60:3 [H 5]), of Babylon's judgment (Jer. 51:7), of violence (Prov 4:17) and of desire (Song 1:2; 4:10).

Wine was the most intoxicating drink known in ancient times. All the wine was light wine, i.e. not fortified with extra alcohol. Concentrated alcohol was only known in the Middle Ages when the Arabs invented distillation ("alcohol" is an Arabic word), so what is now called liquor or strong drink (i.e. whisky, gin, etc.) and the twenty percent fortified wines were unknown in Bible times. Beer was brewed by various methods, but its alcoholic content was light. The strength of natural wines is limited by two factors. The percentage of alcohol will be half of the percentage of the sugar in the juice. And if the alcoholic content is much above 10 or 11 percent, the yeast cells are killed and fermentation ceases. Probably ancient wines were about 7–10 percent. Drunkenness is therefore suggested to be an ancient curse, but alcoholism was not as common or as severe as it is today. And in an agricultural age, its effects were less deadly than now. Still, even then, it had its dangers and Prov 20:1 and 23:29–35 are emphatic in their warnings. To avoid drunkenness, mingling of wine with water was practised. This dilution was specified by the Rabbis in New Testament times' for the wine then customary at Passover. The original Passover did not include wine (Deut 20:6).[65]

Skar

This verb does not appear often and is used nineteen times in the Old Testament, twelve of which are in the prophetic books. James Holding notes that the word translated in the KJV as "strong drink" is derived from a root meaning to be tipsy and is thus associated with strong alcoholic drink. Thus, for Holding, *aekar* is an intoxicant.[66]

With very few exceptions, *aekar* and its derivatives are used

---

[65] Harris, Archer and Waltke. *Theological Wordbook.*
[66] Holding, *A Little Whine.*

in a highly unfavourable and negative context. But the few passages where the root is used in an acceptable sense should be observed. Genesis 43:34, says of Joseph's brothers that they literally "drank and 'became drunk' with him" ("were merry with him"). The emphasis is on conviviality, not drinking to the point of drunkenness. Second, "strong drink" was to be used in the drink offering (Num 28:7) which, of course, was not drunk, but poured out as a libation. Third, the annual tithe to be paid to the Lord, the owner of the soil, might involve strong drink (Deut 14:26). Fourth, *aekar* could be used as a stimulant; Prov 31:6 says, "Give strong drink unto him that is about to perish" (and cf. Mt 27:34; Mk 15:23). At the cross, however, the AV of Mt 27:34 says Jesus refused the vinegar, but the better texts call it wine. He accepted the (dilute) vinegar later (Mt 27:48). Fifth, at Song 5:1 it is suggested to be lovely and put together with milk and honey. Thus, of almost sixty uses of the root *aekar*, only five refer to something good and acceptable.

Several instances of intoxication, caused by *aekar*, are noted in Scripture: (i) Gen 9:20–27, Noah; (ii) I Sam 25:36, Nabal; (iii) II Sam 13:28–29, Amnon; (iv) I Kgs 16:9, Elah; (v) I Kgs 20:16, Benhadad. Of special interest are those passages which indicate that God sends drunkenness upon people. So, Jer 13:13 says, "I am going to fill with drunkenness (kings, prophets, and priests)," or Is 63:6, "I will make them drunk in my fury." These passages employ anthropomorphic and metaphorical ways of writing about God. Thus, to say "God sends drunkenness" is a metaphor for God's presumed punishment. The idea is that drunkenness indicates helplessness. Thus, God says to his people (Is 49:26), "I will make your oppressors eat their flesh and they shall be drunk with their own blood." Here, "to be drunken" means "to be helpless,"· "I will reduce your oppressors to a state of total helplessness" (Cf. Jer 25:27; 51:39, 57). It is therefore no doubt that *sekar* refers to strong drink or beer and often appears in connection with *yayin*.[67]

Tiyrowsh

This word, translated "wine" in the KJV and "new wine" in some newer versions refers to the initial squeezing of juice from

---

[67] Harris, Archer and Waltke. *Theological Wordbook.*

the grape. Holding notes that it is rarely used of fermented wine. Its newness is confirmed by its application as part of the first fruits dedicated to God (Deut. 14:23) and by its grouping with agricultural products as a victim of drought (Hag. 1:1). The term itself suggests something non-alcoholic.[68]

In the New Testament, *oinos* and *gleukos* are the two Greek words that are of interest. *Oinos,* the most used word did not have to mean something intoxicating. It is often used to refer to unfermented grape juice. This does not still rule out its occasional use to refer to strong drink. The mention of the bursting of the wineskins, Matt 9:17; Mk 2:22; Lk 5:37, implies fermentation. See also Eph 5:18.

The drinking of wine could be a stumbling block and for this reason, the apostle Paul enjoins abstinence in this respect, as in others, so as to avoid giving occasion of stumbling to a brother or sister. Rom 14:21 contrasts 1 Tim 5:23 which has an entirely different connection. In this case, the use of wine was entirely for medicinal purposes. The word, *oinos* is also used metaphorically; (a) of the evils ministered to the nations by religious Babylon, Rev 14:8; 17:2; 18:3; (b) of the contents of the cup of Divine wrath upon the nations and Babylon, Rev 14:10; 16:19; 19:15.

The word, *gleukos,* however, denotes sweet or "new wine." The reference in Acts 2:13 where the accusation refers to an intoxicant suggests, however, that *"gleukos* must have been undergoing fermentation for some time."[69]

Though these reflections on the use of wine in the Bible may suggest some ambivalence, it is worth noting that inasmuch as there are occasions of proper use of wine in the Bible, its abuse and drunkenness are clearly forbidden.

Theological Views on Alcohol

A cursory look at the various theological orientations and debates clearly suggest two main views of alcohol. These views are clearly based on moderation or abstinence. I will at this point reflect briefly on four theological perspectives as presented by: (i) Calvin and the Reformed traditions, (ii) Wesley and the Methodist

---

[68] Holding, *A Little Whine.*

[69] See W. E. Vine. *An Expository Dictionary of New Testament Words* . Old Tappan, NJ: Femin H. Rovell Co., 1966, pp. 219-220.

traditions, (iii) Lutheranism and (iv) the more recent Assemblies of God tradition.

Calvin and the Reformed Traditions

Considering Calvin's commentary on Psalm 104:15,[70] *"And wine that cheereth the heart of man,"* one is confronted with the introduction:

> In these words we are taught, that God not only provides for men's necessity, and bestows upon them as much as is sufficient for the ordinary purposes of life, but that in his goodness he deals still more bountifully with them by cheering their hearts with wine and oil. Nature would certainly be satisfied with water to drink; and therefore the addition of wine is owing to God's superabundant liberality.

This seems to suggest that for Calvin, wine is good and must be used as a blessing from God, suggesting that "God not only bestows upon men what is sufficient for their moderate use, but that he goes beyond this, giving them even their delicacies." However, people ought to take care not to abuse God's benefits by giving way to excess. Calvin further notes that "as God bountifully provides for us, so he has appointed a law of temperance, that each may voluntarily restrain himself in his abundance." For Calvin therefore, the more bountiful God is towards humans, the more they ought to take care not to pollute, by their intemperance, the abundance which is presented before them. Thus, Calvin proposes an observance of the rules of moderation so that humankind may not ravenously devour God's benefits.

> The proper rule with respect to the use of bodily sustenance is to partake of it that it may sustain, but not oppress us. As the prophet in this account of the divine goodness in providence makes no reference to the excesses of men, we gather from his words that it is lawful to use wine not only in cases of necessity, but also thereby to make us merry. This mirth must however be tempered with sobriety, first,

---

[70] John Calvin. *Commentary on the Book of Psalms,* James Anderson, trans. Grand Rapids: Christian Classics Ethereal Library. http://www.ccel.org/ccel/Calvin/Calcom11.xiii.iii.html.

that men may not forget themselves, drown their senses, and destroy their strength, but rejoice before their God, according to the injunction of Moses (Leviticus 23:40) and, secondly, that they may exhilarate their minds under a sense of gratitude, so as to be rendered more active in the service of God. He who rejoices in this way will also be always prepared to endure sadness, whenever God is pleased to send it. That rule of Paul ought to be kept in mind (Philippians 4:12) "I have learned to abound — I have learned to suffer want."[71]

As one reflects on the position of the Presbyterian Church (USA),[72] Calvin's view is clearly seen as influencing the Presbyterian or Reformed traditions. The former United Presbyterian Church (UPC) in North America was a temperance church advocating total abstinence right up until its absorption into the new UPCUSA in 1957. The PCUS and PCUSA in the 1940s and 1950s supported the goal of voluntary abstinence as a worthy goal in relation to alcohol. The 1961 statement of the UPCUSA Assembly on "The Church and the Problem of Alcohol" provided the first comprehensive statement on the subject which recognizes the fact that many Presbyterians do drink and suggests that the problems of alcohol could be resolved by responsible drinking for those who choose to drink and abstinence for others. In 1986, the reunited church adopted the following statement which invariably reflects the general position of the Presbyterian Church:

> The General Assembly of the Presbyterian Church (USA) does not advocate the prohibition of alcohol, a policy which would appear to attribute the entire problem to alcohol itself. Responsible and non-problematic uses of alcohol have been part of human experience and the Judeo-Christian heritage since the beginning of recorded history. The considerable risks and immense suffering that follow from excessive and unwise uses of alcohol do, however, impose upon all Christians individually and corporately the responsibility to make and encourage judicious and well-informed choices regarding personal and social uses of alcohol.

---

[71] Calvin, *Commentary on Psalms.*
[72] http://www.pcusa.org/101/101-alcohol.htm.

To this end, the General Assembly encourages and supports the personal decision to abstain from alcohol. For those who choose to drink and can do so without becoming dependent, the General Assembly urges a pattern of moderate and responsible drinking behaviour.

In the Reformed Church in America (RCA),[73] it is suggested that according to Scripture, all Christians must avoid drunkenness. For them, though abstinence from alcohol is a morally creditable choice, those who, in their freedom in Christ, choose to use alcohol moderately are not to be condemned. The church should provide pastoral care and guidance for alcoholic church members and their families, including intervention and discipline when necessary.[74]

This suggests that the Presbyterian and Reformed traditions do not oppose moderate drinking but clearly discourages heavy drinking as a matter of principle due to its potential risk to persons and society inherent in its use. In the light of what has been learned about the risks involved in the use of beverages containing alcohol, congregations have been challenged to examine the traditional practice of using wine in the sacrament of Holy Communion. Many churches are choosing to use grape juice out of deference to those with alcohol problems.

Wesley and the Methodist Traditions[75]

In *The Essentials of Methodist Doctrine,* Ted Campbell[76] suggests that Methodists were passionately concerned with the issue of temperance in the use of alcoholic beverages. At first, this meant

---

[73] www.rca.org/NETCOMMMUNITY/page.aspx?&pid=495&srcid=491.

[74] Synod 1984 appointed a study committee to provide pastoral guidelines regarding the use and abuse of and addiction to alcohol and other drugs in response to three overtures from Classes Grand Rapids North, Red Mesa, and Rocky Mountain. Its report was adopted by Synod 1986 and recommended to the churches. Included in the report are guidelines for the responsible use of alcohol, intervention with alcoholics, prevention of alcohol abuse, and discipline of clergy and church employees who struggle with alcohol use. An appendix entitled "Similarities and Differences between Alcoholism and Addiction to Other Drugs" was approved in 1987.

[75] Methodist Tradition here refers to the African Methodist Episcopal (AME), African Methodist Episcopal Zion (AMEZ), The Christian Methodist Episcopal (CME) and the United Methodist Church (UMC) churches.

[76] Ted A. Campbell. *Methodist Doctrine: The Essentials.* Nashville: Abingdon Press, 1999 pp. 91, 92.

quite literally temperance, that is, only weaker (non-distilled) alcoholic beverages could be consumed, and these in strict moderation. Thus, the General Rules of the United Societies[77] clearly forbid "drunkenness: buying or selling spirituous liquors, or drinking them, unless in cases of extreme necessity."[78] However, in eighteenth century use, "spirituous liquors" referred to distilled beverages such as whisky or gin. Eventually, Methodists' experience with the dangers of alcohol led them to recommend total abstinence from alcoholic beverages. It is to this end that Methodists are noted to have involved themselves whole-heartedly in the struggle for prohibition of alcoholic beverages in the United States, believing that the proscription of alcohol would improve the whole of society.

Consequently, the AME Zion Church alters the General Rules at this point prohibiting "spirituous or intoxicating liquors," making clear its commitment to total abstinence. This is furthermore affirmed by way of special advice in the Book of Discipline which has a section on temperance.

> We believe that temperance implies the subordination of all the emotions, passions, and appetites to the control of reason and conscience, and a wise use of suitable articles of food and drink. The Holy Scriptures teach us to abstain from all alcoholic liquors. The manufacturing, buying, selling and using of spirituous liquors is both contrary to Scripture, and against the principles of morality and the public welfare. We most heartily approve of all lawful and Christian efforts to exterminate the traffic, and to save society from the evil results of intemperance, and earnestly advise our people to cooperate in all reasonable measures to put an end to the liquor traffic, and urge a strict observance of temperance by all our members.[79]

---

[77] The General Rules were drawn up by John Wesley in 1743 and functioned as a kind of contract by which members of early Methodist Societies agreed to hold each other accountable for specific moral behaviours (under the three categories of "doing good of all kinds," "avoiding evil of all kinds," and "attending upon the ordinances of God.)" See Campbell, p. 117.

[78] The expression, "cases of extreme necessity" has reference to medicinal uses of distilled beverages.

[79] *AME Zion Book of Discipline*, Chapter IV, paragraph 85.

Lutheranism

Luther's position on the use of alcohol and alcoholism is not quite clear. Though he is believed to be of the same orientation as Calvin in proposing moderation for those who choose to drink,[80] his response to Question 54 in *Luther's Small Catechism*,[81] still raises questions:

> *Question:* What does God require of us in the fifth command-
> ment?

> *Answer:* The third of Luther's responses to the question
> was: We should avoid and assist our neighbour
> in avoiding the abuse of drugs and the use of any
> substance that harms the body and the mind.

Though one is very much aware of the dangerous effects of alcohol as a mood-altering substance, one is still left wondering to what degree Luther would include alcohol in this response. It is, however, worth noting that Luther had no compunction about the use of alcohol, beer in particular.[82]

Assemblies of God Tradition[83]

The General Council of the Assemblies of God has historically opposed the consumption of alcohol in any form. Early documents of the church declare, without reservation or compromise, a position of total abstinence:

> For two reasons we urge all believers to avoid the Satanic
> tool of alcohol which destroys lives, damns souls, and blights
> society: (1) A studied review of the Scriptures affirms a stern
> warning against intoxicating drink and a call to separation
> from this evil for the purpose of better service to God and

[80] See Jim West. *Drinking With Calvin and Luther: A History of Alcohol in the Church.* Lincoln, California: Oakdown, 2003.
[81] *Luther's Small Catechism With Explanation.* St. Louis: Concordia Publishing House, 1991 p. 78.
[82] *Book of Catechisms.* Reference Edition. Louisville, KY: Geneva Press, 2001.
[83] The General Council of the Assemblies of God (Springfield, MO C. 2007). http://ag.org/top/Beliefs/Position_Papers/pp_4187_abstinence.cfm.

mankind; and (2) Current social abuses and the public outrage over the high cost of alcohol in terms of human misery, death, and destruction of property cry out with urgency for the church of Jesus Christ to oppose firmly any use whatsoever of a beverage which so insidiously afflicts and binds the bodies and minds of men and women.

Furthermore, based on record from scriptures on the tragedies caused by alcohol, principles and examples that recommend abstinence, and also God's call to holiness, the Assemblies of God emphasize that the use of alcohol weakens the Christian testimony. For them, moderation is not acceptable since a little alcohol is still too much. This is because "no alcoholic ever intended to become an alcoholic when he/she took the first drink. And no individual who persistently refused to take the first drink ever became an alcoholic."[84] It is therefore suggested that the individual who refuses to have anything to do with such a dangerous taskmaster (alcohol) is wise indeed. To this end, the Assemblies of God affirm that the church of Jesus Christ must take a bold stand against this evil that in the end "bites like a serpent, and stings like a viper" (Proverbs 23:32, NKJV). They thereby make a stringent call to abstinence:

Alcoholic beverages should have no place in the life of the Christian. Let there be no doubt about the Assemblies of God stand on this critical issue. We declare unequivocally our conviction that total abstinence from alcoholic beverages is the only acceptable way of life for the Christian. We call upon every member and adherent in our Fellowship, including both the ministry and the laity, to teach by word and example a life-style that abstains totally from the consumption of alcoholic beverages.

In a review of Kenneth Gentry's *God Gave Wine: What the Bible Says About Alcohol*, Eric Wait summarizes Gentry as suggesting that there are three approaches to this debate. The prohibitionist approach "maintains that Christians should avoid alcoholic beverages as unfit for human consumption." Secondly, the abstentionist approach which "maintains that although

---

[84] The General Council of the Assemblies of God. http://ag.org/top/Beliefs/Position_Papers/pp_4187_abstinence.cfm.

scripture does not expressly forbid alcoholic beverages *in toto*, alcohol consumption in our society today is nevertheless imprudent and should not be condoned." The third position, which Gentry defends, is the moderationist view which maintains that alcoholic beverages are permitted to Christians if moderately consumed and in a circumspect manner.[85]

These biblical and theological reflections suggest that even though God gave wine, its use and abuse is subject to much debate. This notwithstanding, it is however worth noting that the consumption of alcohol, in many instances, has become a national crisis, destroying families and tearing at the moral fabric of every nation. Christians cannot meet their moral responsibilities by a posture of neutrality about alcohol. The problem is not merely economic, cultural, or social. In the final analysis, the use of alcohol is a spiritual problem and this is evident in the shocking spiritual degeneration confronting our society today due to alcohol use and abuse. It is for this reason that Professor Christopher Cook contends that Christian theology does have an important contribution to make to an understanding of addictive disorders, particularly to an understanding of the ethics of alcohol use and misuse. However, according to Professor Cook, this contribution is best appreciated not by a narrow focus on scriptural texts making explicit references to drunkenness, but rather by broader theological reflection on the phenomenon of alcohol dependence and addiction.[86]

Is Alcoholism a Disease or a Sin?

Hitherto, the earlier reflections in this chapter have sought to advocate Jellinek's disease concept of alcoholism since it is more embracing and reflective of the nature of alcoholism as a chronic, progressive ailment. It has also been contended that the "wholistic" model which seeks not to deconstruct the disease concept but to suggest that in emphasizing the disease concept as well as spiritual/mystical causality, one should not lose sight of the moral, psychological, genetic transmission, temperance, environmental and social education models and their

---

[85] www.ericwait.com. 31 March, 2006. See also, Kenneth L. Gentry Jr., *God Gave Wine: What the Bible Says About Alcohol*. Oakdown: Lincoln, 2001.

[86] Christopher Cook. "A Theology of the Use and Misuse of Alcohol," www.ias.org.uk.

contribution to understanding the concept of alcoholism. This is because they all influence its development and manifestation in one way or the other. For the African, the place of "spiritual forces" as agents of causation of this problem must be emphasized.

However, most Christian traditions view the issue of alcoholism as a moral issue and contend, as in Galatians 5:19-21, that drunkenness is clearly immoral and forbidden altogether in the Bible.[87] The church is, however, seen as considering the issue of alcoholism with all seriousness in view of the fact that alcohol abuse and addiction is said to be involved in most conflicts and misunderstandings, murders, assaults, child abuse cases, traffic fatalities, and most fire and drowning accidents, which are all perversions of societal and Christian standards.

As emphasized earlier in this chapter, while the alcoholic drinks involuntarily, the alcohol abuser chooses to get drunk. The alcoholic cannot resist his/her craving for alcohol because one's willpower is in service to the addiction. According to Spickard and Thompson, "telling an alcoholic to shape up is like telling a man who jumps out of a nine-story building to fall only three floors. Words will not alter the inevitable outcome." Due to the helplessness or vulnerability of the alcoholic and the predictable progressive nature of alcoholism, coupled with the inheritance or genetic factor, it will be appropriate to describe alcoholism as an illness or a disease. However, it is not simply a physical disease but a "paradigm disease of the whole person."[88] It is a sickness which is not limited to one part of the body but encompasses the whole body; mind, spirit, emotions, and also relationships. For James Royce, considering alcoholism as a disease must not be construed too narrowly. "It must be considered as a physiological, psychological, and spiritual illness: the whole person is sick."[89]

---

[87] *The acts of the sinful nature are obvious: sexual immorality, impurity and debauchery; idolatry and witchcraft; hatred, discord, jealousy, fits of rage, selfish ambition, dissentions, factions and envy; drunkenness, orgies and the like. I warn you, as I did before, that those who live like this will not inherit the kingdom of God* (Gal 5:19-21) (emphasis mine).

[88] Spickard and Thompson, *Dying for a Drink*, p. 41.

[89] James E. Royce, S.J. "Alcohol and Other Drug Dependencies," in *Clinical Handbook of Pastoral Counselling*, Volume 1, Expanded Edition, edited by Robert J. Wicks, Richard D. Parsons and Donald Capps, Mahwah, NJ: Paulist Press, 1993, p. 503.

Addiction has a life of its own and the alcoholic has therefore "set in motion powerful forces over which he has no control." This affirms the ancient saying, "first the man takes a drink, then the drink takes a drink, then the drink takes the man."[90] Consequently, the alcoholic begins to demonstrate predictable but often unrecognized symptoms of addiction. Thus, even though from the Christian point of view, drunkenness in any form and in its development is generally characterized as a sin and viewed as being a result of moral and spiritual deviation, the nature, form, and characteristics of alcoholism as a chronic, progressive and fatal phenomenon, seeks to suggest its nature as a disease. Treatment modules must therefore embrace the physiological and psychological, but without ignoring the theological or spiritual.

> Since the drinking of alcoholics is not a matter of choice but the symptom of a disease, there is no use in appealing to goodwill or exhorting them to use will power. That is like telling a tubercular patient not to cough. Drunkenness is a sin, of course, for those who deliberately choose it. But alcoholics do not choose to get drunk; they get drunk in spite of intending not to. They are not morally depraved. They are sick. They are sinners, but aren't we all?[91]

We can herein surmise from the foregoing that alcohol abuse can be described as a sin, but alcoholism or alcohol addiction is a disease. As one considers this debate, it is worth asking whether people who get drunk are exercising their illegitimate rights or behaving irresponsibly. For Professor Cook, the "moral model" which is generally endorsed by Christendom has become the subject of much criticism in scientific and medical circles. The more enlightened view is to understand the addict as sick rather than sinful. However, whether viewed as an illness from the enlightenment perspective or as a sin from the Christian perspective of some people, it is widely acknowledged that spirituality, and for that matter theology, largely as a result of the work of Alcoholics Anonymous and its sister organizations, is increasingly considered to be vital to providing wholistic

---

[90] Spickard and Thompson, *Dying for a Drink*, p. 41.
[91] Royce, *Alcohol and Other Drug Dependencies*, p. 512.

treatment and alcoholism is viewed by many as being a spiritual problem.[92] To this end, freedom for the addict can only be a matter of the grace of God in Jesus Christ. This therefore calls for an assurance of hope, faith and love for the addict as one seeks freedom from the subjective compulsion to use alcohol.

Effects of Alcoholism

As a disease that affects the "whole person," not leaving out families and communities, the effects of alcoholism are quite devastating. Though its consequences are generally noted as being negative, for Kraft, there are certain positive consequences. This, however, is still no justification for drinking excessively. Kraft therefore asserts that "if there were no negative consequences, drinking alcoholically might be justified."[93] Thus, whatever positive gains might be derived from alcoholism, they fail to foster ongoing healthy growth. "They are short term gains that lead to long term losses."[94] The overwhelming negative consequences ultimately outweigh whatever positive gain one attains. It is worth emphasizing that people generally seem to be *ambivalent* about the use of alcohol: on the one hand, it is pleasurable, provides social conviviality, and on the other hand, it is seen as disgusting and degrading. Whichever way one looks at it all *depends on the experience of the person;* whether negative or positive, and it is from this that our attitudes and conclusions are drawn accordingly.

Positive Consequences

According to Kraft, "alcoholics drink because it makes sense." This is because they feel better when drinking even though this "good" feeling is for a short while. Alcohol tends to offer some sense of fulfillment and makes one experience a sense of serenity, albeit a "pseudo-sense that neither lasts nor is freely engendered from within themselves."[95] Nevertheless, alcohol gives a counterfeit feeling of peace, calm, and comfort which suggests that "when drinking, everything is on euphoric hold."[96] As a

---

[92] Christopher Cook. "A Theology of the Use and Misuse of Alcohol."
[93] Kraft, *Normal Alcoholic*, p. 81.
[94] Kraft, *Normal Alcoholic*, p. 25.
[95] Kraft, *Normal Alcoholic*, p. 81.
[96] Kraft, *Normal Alcoholic*, p. 82.

result, to become sober one must endeavour to face and replace alcoholically-induced illusions with healthy and more realistic experiences.

With the illusion that alcohol is a stimulant, alcohol can also give an illusion of health and make certain people feel more "confident, freer, and assertive" while others also feel they are "more imaginative, spontaneous, and creative."[97] This could be due to the fact that alcohol numbs one's conscience and the drinker "feels freer" to act in ways that are normally forbidden. Alcohol thus becomes a catalyst for expressing feelings that are normally repressed and also serves as a stress and pain reducer for reducing any feelings of discomfort. It can be surmised herein that whatever relief one seeks to derive from drinking are temporary and "true serenity is absent." Thus, to become sober, "alcoholic sense must be replaced with sober sense."[98] An understanding of the negative consequences is therefore relevant in order to persuade drinkers to overcome the decline that alcohol abuse brings on them.

Negative Consequences

Despite the fact that culture is suggested as influencing drinking patterns, the physiological and mental effects of alcohol addiction appear to be universal, although tolerance levels vary for individuals, and rates of metabolism may also vary among men and women.[99] Despite its functionality in many instances facilitating community building and emphasizing social hierarchy, its dysfunctional effects on the individual and community at large are enormous.[100] Alcohol more or less affects all aspects of life. Once consumed it initially lessens inhibitions and gives a sense of liberation. It, however, quickly acts as a depressant that impairs and numbs one's physical, cognitive, affective, social and spiritual functions and slows one down because it affects the brain and other parts of the nervous system. Though most of these effects may be physical, the psycho-social

---

[97] Kraft, *Normal Alcoholic*, p. 83.

[98] Kraft, *Normal Alcoholic*, p. 83.

[99] See David G. Mandelbaum. "Alcohol and Culture," *Current Anthropology* 6, 3 (1965) p. 281-293.

[100] Emmanuel Akyeampong. *Drink, Power, and Cultural Change: A Social History of Alcohol in Ghana, c. 1800 to Recent Times.* Portsmouth, NH: Heinemann 1996, p. 3ff.

and spiritual effects are significantly devastating.

It has been noted that the liver breaks down alcohol in the body and is therefore the chief site of alcohol damage. Liver damage could result in fatty liver, alcoholic hepatitis and cirrhosis. A diseased liver cannot convert stored glycogen into glucose, thus lowering blood sugar and producing hypoglycemia. It cannot manufacture bile (*for fat digestion*), prothrombin (*for blood clotting and bruise prevention*), and albumin (*for maintaining healthy cells*).[101]

Alcohol disturbs the structure and functions of the central nervous system profoundly by disrupting the ability to retrieve and consolidate information. This could affect cognitive abilities and also cause "blackout" during drunkenness. It also causes brain damage and a neurological disorder sometimes referred to as *Wernicke-Korsakoff's Syndrome*, which is a result of the direct action of alcohol on the brain. This leads to one having symptoms such as amnesia, short-term loss of memory, disorientation, hallucinations, emotional disturbances, double vision, and loss of muscle control.

Alcohol use in large quantities could inflame the mouth, oesophagus and stomach; thus causing cancer in these locations. It also produces heartburn, nausea, gastritis and ulcers. The intestines may be inflamed, leading to sluggish digestion and vomiting. High blood pressure, heart attacks, heart arrhythmia and heart disease are some effects of alcohol on the heart. Even though it has generally been reported that moderate drinking may be good for the heart, "one binge may produce irregular heart beats."[102]

Fetal Alcohol Syndrome (FAS) is a cluster of irreversible birth abnormalities that are the direct results of heavy drinking during pregnancy and affects the unborn child who may suffer symptoms even after the alcohol is no longer present. This may eventually cause such children to be born with certain physical abnormalities or defects. Pregnant women are therefore advised to endeavour to totally abstain from alcoholic beverages.

Since alcohol quickly depresses inhibitions and judgements, the drinker may feel friendlier, more gregarious and more expansive as inhibitions are released, hence the often used suggestion to *have a drink and loosen up*. Sexual desire may also

---

[101] http://www.family-drug-intervention.net/alcohol and_health.html.
[102] http://www.family-drug-intervention.net/alcohol and_health.html.

be enhanced, thus giving alcohol the reputation as an aphrodisiac, but in reality, alcohol rather impairs sexual function and performance, and eventually blunts desire. Radical mood changes such as bouncing from euphoria to self-pity and even weeping are also typical characteristics of intoxication.

Alcohol adversely affects motor ability, muscle function, reaction time, eyesight, depth perception, and night vision. Carnage on the highway is largely a result of drinking. It is for this reason that we have the common slogan used in everyday language which says, *"If you drink don't drive, and if you drive don't drink."* This is because those abilities are needed to operate a motor vehicle. Since alcohol depresses the heart and lung function, it slows down breathing and circulation. This could eventually lead to death if alcohol completely paralyzes breathing or circulation.

A hangover, which is generally characterized as a withdrawal state, normally results in headaches, upset stomach, dehydration, etc. Though people tend to medicate this withdrawal state with more alcohol, the best prevention for hangover is abstinence. Other withdrawal symptoms are anxiety, depressed mood or depression, malaise or weakness, autonomic hyperactivity, tachycardia, sweating, elevated blood pressure, orthostatic hypotension, coarse tremor of hands, tongue, and eyelids.

On the other hand, other effects include mental disorders such as increased aggression, antisocial behaviour, depression and anxiety. These overwhelming physical and mental effects in general are due to the fact that alcohol easily permeates every cell and organ of the body, while the numerous psychological and emotional effects could also lead to suicidal thoughts and eventual death. It has been noted that the negative ramifications of all the other psycho-active drugs put together cannot measure up to the medical ramifications of alcohol. This is because alcohol abuse or dependence is the cause of at least 18 or 19 medical complications.

Although alcoholics can live spiritually, they are in constant conflict since alcohol tends to be a replacement for God. This is to suggest that, with alcoholism, "God is displaced as the center of life," and alcohol thus becomes the "saving grace."[103] This

---

[103] Kraft, *Normal Alcoholic*, p. 95.

reflects one's powerlessness over alcohol and over oneself. For the alcoholic, to be able to admit his/her powerlessness, one must endeavour to surrender unto a higher power which leads him/her to consequently replace one's alcoholic sense with a healthy sense through a reflection on the immediate and long-term negative consequences of drinking.

Most alcoholics are noted not to think themselves into right acting, nor thinking, even though in doing this, one is more likely to maintain and foster sobriety and evince less desire to drink.

Despite the health and psychological effects, as well as the spiritual impairment, the socio-economic effects on the family and society cannot go without mention. In the book, *Alcohol Use and Abuse: Reports and Recommendations of the Presbyterian Church (USA)*, we find "it is estimated that for each individual who experiences personal problems related to his or her own drinking, three others are directly and adversely affected."[104] This emphasizes the problem of alcoholism as a family disease. It has also been suggested that more than half of all adults have a family history of alcoholism or problem drinking and in America, more than nine million children live with a parent dependent on alcohol and/or illicit drugs.[105] Also, untreated addiction is said to be more expensive than heart disease, diabetes and cancer combined. These and other alcohol induced occupational problems suggest that economic costs attached to alcohol abuse to the society are quite crushing.

Alcoholism in the Family

Though the aforementioned consequences seem to reflect more on the individual alcoholic, its momentous downbeat effects on the family must by no means be consigned to silence. According to Martin Doot, families become alcoholic too. He suggests that the problem with alcoholism is that it does not just affect individuals, it engulfs entire families and that children in families with an alcoholic parent are admitted to hospitals 25 percent more often than other children. Also, persons with alcoholism and their families need supportive health care at rates two or

---

[104] PCUSA, *Alcohol Use and Abuse: The Social and Health Effects*, p. 14.
[105] http://www.family-drug-intervention.net/alcoholism.html.

three times higher than comparable families of similar size and age ranges.[106]

For Royce, alcoholism is a family disease in that, "the spouse and family need help as much as or more than the alcoholic."[107] Though this family illness may not be the same as alcoholism, it can be just as devastating. Shame, guilt, fear, isolation, and loss are significant contexts in which families are entangled, making their affliction legion; suggesting that the progression of alcoholism often engulfs entire families in a perpetual nightmare. Thus, when one's family is suffering from any individual alcoholic, the whole family is not only affected but involved; not only psycho-socially, physically and emotionally, but also spiritually. Thus, alcoholism as a family illness is basically due to the "tremendous impact those with active alcohol dependence have on those around them."[108]

This suggests that it is very difficult, if not impossible, for family members to escape the impact of an individual alcoholic member in the day to day interactions of the family. This generally renders the family as dysfunctional as the individual alcoholic member.

Even though there are several ways that the family responds to alcoholism, one significant form of manifestation of the crises that both family members and alcoholics go through is the process of denial and its concomitant phenomenon of a conspiracy of silence and isolation within the family and the larger social system.

> Alcoholism is known as a disease of denial, whose chief symptom is inability to see that one has it. We say inability rather than unwillingness, for this is not denial in the sense of any rational, conscious rejection of the idea but an emotional blocking which is largely subconscious. This denial has been called 'honest self-deception.'[109]

This is, however, not limited to the individual but involves the family and society, including professionals. Thus, denial is noted as a fundamental obstruction to alcoholism. Once the problem

---

[106] Dejong and Doot. *Dying for a Drink*, p. 8.
[107] Royce, *Alcohol and Other Drug Dependencies*, p. 516.
[108] Jean Kinney. *Loosening the Grip: A Handbook of Alcohol Information*, Seventh edition. New York, N.Y.: McGraw Hill, 2003, p. 198.
[109] Royce, *Alcohol and Other Drug Dependencies*, p. 503.

is being denied by the patient, he/she tends to reject all efforts to correct this flaw. This experience, according to Albers, is influenced by shame. Generally, the pervasive nature of shame in addiction is a dynamic that turns denial into a systemic conspiracy of silence and isolation.[110] Contemplation on shame and its dynamics at this point will certainly offer us an understanding of the constellation of defence mechanisms that individuals and family members employ for survival, though it rather disrupts and cripples life as it fuels the addiction.

Shame and its Perpetuation of Denial

Though shame could be positive or negative, for the purpose of this chapter, its positive dynamic will not be emphasized since the negatives invariably outweigh the positives as it cripples life out of the persons engulfed by it.[111] Several writers have attempted to provide a definition as to what shame is and what it is not. In the *New Dictionary of Pastoral Studies*, shame is defined as "a painful emotional state of humiliation caused by the exposure, or the fear of exposure, of failure or deficiency."[112] Stephen Pattison asserts that it is an acute sense of unwanted exposure, followed by an urgent desire to cover oneself.[113] According to Lewis Smedes, shame is a very heavy feeling, "a feeling that we do not measure up and maybe never will measure up to the sort of persons we are meant to be."[114]

Kaufman, however, identifies shame, first of all, as "an

---

[110] Robert H. Albers. "Shame and the Conspiracy of Silence," *Journal of Ministry in Addiction and Recovery*, Vol. 7(1) 2000, Robert Albers, Editor. The Haworth Press, Inc. 2000, p. 51f.

[111] Albers, quoting Carl Schneider and Donald Nathanson, refers to the positive dynamic of shame as "discretionary shame" and identifies the negative form as "disgrace shame." John Bradshaw in *Healing the Shame that Binds Us* however refers to this positive dynamic as "nourishing or healthy shame," and to the negative as "toxic shame." For the purpose of this chapter, the writer will simply use Gershen Kaufman's reference to shame as used and refer to either disgrace or toxic shame as a phenomenon which is unhealthy for the human condition.

[112] Wesley Carr et al., eds. *The New Dictionary of Pastoral Studies*. Grand Rapids, Michigan: W.B. Eerdmans Publishing Co., 2002, p. 336.

[113] Stephen Pattison. *Shame: Theory, Therapy, Theology*. Cambridge, UK: Cambridge University Press, 2000, p. 40.

[114] Lewis Smedes. *Shame and Grace: Healing the Shame We Don't Deserve*. Harper San Francisco: Zondervan Publishing House p. 5.

affect, an emotion or feeling."[115] It is an acute sense of exposure, being seen as basically deficient in some fundamental aspect of being human, accompanied by a feeling of powerlessness. [116] Kaufman vividly captures the inner experience of shame when he states:

> To feel shame is to feel seen in a painfully diminished sense. The self feels exposed both to itself and to anyone else present. It is this sudden, unexpected feeling of exposure and accompanying self-consciousness that characterize the essential nature of the effect of shame. Contained in the experience of shame is that piercing awareness of ourselves as fundamentally deficient in some vital way as a human being. To live with shame is to experience the very essence or heart of the self as wanting. [117]

This is to suggest that shame can have a very debilitating and crippling effect on the individual. It is such that it makes one see oneself as fundamentally flawed as an individual. This state of being, according to Kaufman, is an impotence-making experience.

> Shame is an impotence-making experience because it feels as though there is no way to relieve the matter, no way to restore the balance of things. One has simply failed as a human being. No single action is seen as wrong and, hence reparable. So, *'there is nothing I can do to make up for it.'* This is impotence.[118]

Whichever way one looks at the above definitions, one can surmise that shame is a feeling one would always want to avoid. There is certainly a fear of exposure and then much energy is spent in service to its concealment. There is fear of being humiliated and embarrassed, fear of despair and anguish, and unbearable self-watchfulness. It is a persistent, unrelenting and

[115] Gershen Kaufman. *Shame: The Power of Caring*, 3rd edition Rochester, Vermont: Schenkman Books Inc. 1992, p. xi.

[116] Deborah Van Deusen Hunsinger. *Theology and Pastoral Counselling: A New Interdisciplinary Approach*. Grand Rapids, Michigan: William Erdman's Publishing Co. 1995, p. 172.

[117] Kaufman, *Shame*, p. 8f.

[118] Kaufman, *Shame*, p. 9.

importunate feeling of being unacceptable, unworthy and of not being a good person in life. This feeling of exposure invariably is seen by others and by one's self as a sense of deficiency. It is a primal feeling that seeps in and discolours all of one's other feelings about oneself and about everyone and everything else in one's life. Consequently, Albers asserts that there are basically two interrelated dynamics present in shame. "One is the exposure or the fear of exposure and the other is a self-conscious awareness of being different from the prevailing norm of acceptability."[119] Shame is invariably a vague undefined heaviness that presses on one's spirit, dampens one's gratitude for the goodness of life, and slackens the free flow of one's joy.[120] Due to its excruciating nature, it is a helpless feeling of defeat and isolation to the extent that even knowing and acknowledging it generates more shame.

Even though Kaufman emphasizes that shame basically originates interpersonally in significant relationships, he also suggests that "it can become internalized so that the self is able to activate shame without an inducing interpersonal event," thus suggesting that "interpersonally induced shame develops into internally induced shame."[121] At this point, one's identity or the vital sense of self-worth as an individual coupled with one's dignity as a human being can be obliterated through lingering shame; leaving one feeling naked, exposed, defeated as a person and unbearably alone.

Human beings are need creatures. According to Kaufman, from the moment of one's birth through to adult life, one is always in need of relationships and groping for mutual acceptance. Due to one's desire to find fulfillment and satisfaction, one accordingly seeks bonding with significant individuals who exhibit love, care and respect for us. A mutual kind of healthy interpersonal bonding based on trust between one and a significant other. This bond, Kaufman describes metaphorically as the *interpersonal bridge*.

> Relationships begin when one person actively reaches out to another and establishes emotional ties . . . such a process entails establishing a bond. In this way, relationships gradually evolve out of reciprocal interest in one another

[119] Albers, *Shame and the Conspiracy of Silence*, p. 53.
[120] Smedes, *Shame and Grace*, p. 5.
[121] Kaufman, *Shame*, p. 8.

along with shared experiences of trust . . . An emotional bond begins to grow between individuals as they communicate understanding, respect, and valuing for one another's personhood, needs, and feelings included . . . This bond which ties two individuals together forms an *interpersonal bridge* between them.[122]

Whenever one experiences a rejection, disapproval, or there is lack of responsiveness to one's needs by the significant other, one feels one's trust being betrayed and the interpersonal bridge is ruptured. At this point, shame occurs. This is because, we feel the "self" ruptured and therefore terribly exposed. Anger or rage at this point is just a defence mechanism against further exposure or humiliation which may in turn induce some amount of shame in the significant other.

Aside from this interpersonal origin, it has also been noted that at any point in the individual's life cycle, shame may originate, thus suggesting developmental origins of shame. It is, however, worth noting that the origination process of shame, primarily, according to Kaufman, involves some kind of breaking of the interpersonal bridge. From earliest childhood through adolescence to adulthood, one experiences the severance of the interpersonal bridge and hence shame. These developmental processes which can be made more manifest in dysfunctional families of origin, shame-based parental models, multigenerational family issues, abandonment issues, school settings, religion and culture, are all critical settings that could perpetuate internalization of shame and hence cause one to manifest "the demonic power of toxic shame."[123] According to Kaufman, when shame is internalized, it becomes one's source of identity. Kaufman describes human beings as generally in need of an identity. The need or strong desire to be accepted as part of a group or society is something bigger than oneself and worthy of one's loyalty. "We long to feel a vital part of some community of others, to have the security that comes through belonging to something larger than ourselves."[124] It is through this process of identification that we ultimately become rooted. This need to

---

[122] Kaufman, *Shame*, p. 13.

[123] Bradshaw, *Healing the Shame*, p. 29.

[124] Kaufman, *Shame*, p. 38.

belong is one of the places we can get caught on the hooks of shame. Couture and Hunter therefore suggest that "a family becomes dysfunctional when it gives its children an identity of shame."[125] This, according to Bradshaw, can be transmitted from generation to generation. Thus, the family is one crucial setting where shame can be perpetuated and be eventually bound up by this phenomenon when it becomes part of its identity. The family not wanting to feel terribly exposed will consequently cover up its feeling of exposure with a set of defence mechanisms including denial. However care must be taken so as not to confuse shame with guilt feelings, especially in relation to alcohol addiction.

Shame vs. Guilt

Guilt is a major problem confronting both alcoholics and family members. It will be erroneous to try to associate shame with guilt. Albers contends that guilt is principally phenomenological in nature while shame is primarily ontological.[126] Teasing out the distinctions, one can say that whereas shame is about the self, guilt is about actions of the self.[127] Guilt relates to what we have done whereas shame relates to what we are — a feeling of moral inadequacy.[128] Shame is more all-encompassing and total, while guilt is partial and related to specific actions. One feels guilty for what one does, whereas one feels shame over one's very being or nature. While guilt will merely say "I did," shame will say, "I did, therefore I am."[129] Guilt has to do with values and does not "reflect directly upon one's identity or diminish one's sense of personal worth."[130] Thus, a guilt feeling can best be described as a painful feeling of regret and responsibility for one's actions, while shame is a painful feeling about one's self as a person. For the shameful person, there is no possibility of repair since it comes as a confirmation of one's negative perceptions of oneself. Guilt on the other hand helps reaffirm

---

[125] Pamela D. Couture and Rodney Hunter. Ed. *Pastoral Care and Social Conflict*, Nashville: Abingdon Press, 1995, p.6.

[126] Albers, *Conspiracy of Silence*, p. 53.

[127] Kaufman, *Shame*, p.xiii.

[128] Hunsinger, *Theology and Pastoral Counselling*, p. 172.

[129] Smedes, *Shame and Grace*, p. 14.

[130] Bradshaw, *Healing the Shame*, p. 17.

one's values which consequently enhances erudition and growth.

Due to its painful, debilitating, destructive and dehumanizing nature, shame is something that everyone would want to avoid because it weighs one's spirits down and crushes out one's joy. This unhealthy feeling of unworthiness that gives a distorted view of oneself, infects the family with a lingering sorrow. Albers suggests that shame perpetuates denial and creates a pall of silence around addiction. The family feels the following: *disgust, deficiency, desertion, dishonor, defectiveness* and *defilement.* Such situations absolutely put undue stress on both individual alcoholics and their families; for Albers, "the power of shame shackles all of the people who are adversely affected by addiction."[131] And all this is because a family member is alcoholic.

Though shame might appear as a psycho-social phenomenon, its physical effects are enormous. Much energy is accordingly spent in keeping it a secret which consequently results in illness even for those affected.

> Respiratory problems, intestinal problems and migraine headaches are only a few of the maladies that can result from stress occasioned by the need to keep silence about someone who is addicted. Yet internally those who are affected suffer the consequences of this devastating pressure and desire to keep things quiet. Disgrace, shame is the culprit that precipitates these physical maladies as the pains of the psyche become somatized for many people.[132]

The impact of shame is not only seen in terms of physical defectiveness but also in terms of the emotional, social and the spiritual. Though time and space will not allow us to enumerate these implications, for the purpose of this study, a cursory reflection on the spiritual defects of shame will be useful. Other manifestations that influence denial include sunken self-esteem, perfectionism and pride.

---

[131] Albers, *Conspiracy of Silence*, p. 53-57, See also Albers, *Shame: A Faith Perspective*. New York: The Haworth Press, 1995.

[132] Albers, *Conspiracy of Silence*, p. 57f.

Shame and Spirituality

Albers asserts that "the shame of having the disease itself takes its toll on the spiritual life of the person afflicted."[133] This is to suggest that one's spiritual life is destroyed by the stigma or shame associated with alcoholism. It causes people to isolate themselves from others as well as from the community of faith; erodes relationship with the ultimate, God; it makes one condemn oneself as doomed and unworthy of divine favour. Thus, the interpersonal relation that is to exist between one and others is broken. With alcoholism, loneliness is a problem. Discouraged, fearful and alienated from others, alcoholics withdraw more and more into the inner self. Alcohol thus becomes their only trusted friend and a source of comfort, even though it betrays them every time.[134] In such depressing situations, hopelessness and helplessness become daily companions as one continues in this relentless and inexorable walk into the jaws of death. This downward degrading trend inevitably affects relationships and infects them with a horrendous spiritual pestilence.

To avoid being ridiculed, isolation becomes a behaviour of choice. While doubt and despair reign supreme, resentment takes the place of relationship, soon family relationships downgrade and break down. In such situations the vertical and horizontal dimensions of one's spirituality are damaged, leading to a culture of silence due to the fear of "losing face" and being shamed.[135] It is therefore noteworthy to concede that at the heart of addiction lies shame. It prompts denial and creates a deadly conspiracy as it shatters families and stifles life out of those affected by the disease.

The critical role of the spiritual dimension in addiction and recovery is therefore very significant. According to Albers, underlying this process of addiction is spirituality that is in jeopardy. This emphasizes that life has become something different from what God intends it to be. For those affected and for the one afflicted, Albers suggests that a three-fold spiritual distress is experienced.[136]

---

[133] Albers, *Conspiracy of Silence*, p. 58.
[134] Royce, *Alcohol and Other Drug Dependencies*, p. 511.
[135] Albers, *Conspiracy of Silence*, p. 60.
[136] Robert H. Albers. "Continuity and Change in the Continuum of Care." *Journal of Ministry in Addiction and Recovery*, Vol. 5(2) 1998, p. 3 .

1. There is the intrapersonal distress of spirit occasioned by the deep internal conflicts which the disease occasions.
2. There is the external stress of interpersonal relationships that are jeopardized or jettisoned as the disease progresses.
3. The transpersonal stress in relationship to God or one's Higher Power.

Albers contends that the spiritual distress on all relational levels is not being taken seriously though spirituality or spiritual dimension is a key principle in the recovery process and must not be relegated or considered as irrelevant. Quoting Paul Tillich, he suggests that unless the core issues in one's spiritual life are addressed, the person(s) afflicted and affected is bereft of an opportunity to discuss those matters which may be most pressing in his/her life. This is because these are issues of "ultimacy" verging on the meaning of life and the reality of death. It is not only the individual alcoholic who is affected, but his/her family too.

> As attempts were employed to monitor, control and preclude the inevitable progression of the addiction, those affected also began to lose hope in the addict, in themselves and in God.[137]

Thus the dysfunctional system needs healing just as much as the dysfunctional individuals within the system. "In essence, one is dealing with a 'community in crisis' since the one addicted affects at a minimum four other persons in her or his social circle."[138] For Hyatt, it is unfortunate that very often, members of the family are viewed as "resources to get the addicted family member better" while the family is denied support, awareness and assistance.[139] The stresses and traumas of family members are often overlooked or given tacit recognition by religious groups, health and treatment facilities, and other agencies within communities. Any therapeutic process without due acknowledgement of the crises within the larger context of the traumas and stresses of the family system, will only tend to be partial and not holistic. Before we proceed to delve into a careful study

---

[137] Albers, *Shame and the Conspiracy of Silence*, p. 59.
[138] Robert H. Albers. "Continuity and Change in the Continuum of Care." *Journal of Ministry in Addiction and Recovery*, Vol. 5(2) 1998, p.3ff.
[139] Hyatt, p. 17.

of family systems theory and how the system functions, it is proper to reflect on the social history and the religio-socio-cultural use of alcohol in Africa, and for that matter Ghana.

Alcohol Use in Africa

As a "legal drug," alcohol use is not illegal and is readily available. In Africa, it plays a very important role in the communal or religio-socio-cultural life of its peoples. Both in the traditional and modern eras, "alcohol and other drug use has been part of the African lifestyle for centuries."[140] It is therefore very rare to see an African gathering or ceremony where alcohol is not used. According to Akyeampong, its centrality is emphasized in the culture of power. Also, since the blessings of the gods and ancestors are regarded as necessary for success and survival, alcohol is used to bridge the gap between the spiritual and living worlds.[141] Though literature on the social history of alcohol in Ghana is very sparse, to be able to understand the meanings people attach to alcohol, it is highly imperative to consider the religio-socio-cultural contexts of the individual and families at large. This is because "social structures, social relations, stress and cultural change impinge on drinking patterns in different societies."[142]

According to Donald Horton, primitive societies used drink to reduce "anxiety" or "fear," suggesting that the level of drunkenness in a society was invariably a reflection of the degree of such stress. For Horton, these feelings of anxiety were alleviated by the release of aggressive impulses during drinking.[143] Horton's assertion has further been confirmed by establishing the correlation between drink and anxiety in both western and non-western societies. In urban Africa, alcohol use

---

[140] Joseph Kow Ghunney. *African Spiritual Worldview: Its Impact on Alcohol and Other Drug Use by Senior Secondary School Students in Ghana.* A dissertation presented in partial fulfillment for the award of the degree of doctor of philosophy. Maryland: Loyola College, April 1994, p. 4.

[141] Akyeampong, *Drink, Power, and Cultural Change.* See also Akyeampong, "Alcohol, Social Conflict and the Struggle for Power in Ghana, 1919 to Recent Times" (PhD dissertation., University of Virginia 1993).

[142] Akyeampong, *Drink, Power, and Cultural Change,* p. 1.

[143] Donald Horton. "The Functions of Alcohol in Primitive Societies: A Cross-Cultural Study," *Quarterly Journal of Studies on Alcohol* 4, 2 (1943), pp. 199-320.

has been attributed largely to economic insecurity.[144] This view, however, as suggested by Horton, ignores the religio-cultural uses of drink in an integrative way and the fact that drinking is not to be seen as a representation of the only medium for reducing stress. This argument therefore seeks to negate the reality that each culture defines its own drinking patterns.[145] Akyeampong contends that the meanings of alcohol, forged within a changing cultural and historical context in southern Ghana, were closely linked to conceptions of power, and by extension disempowerment. We can herein agree with Mary Douglas's assertion, as does Akyeampong that "drink — as a ritual object, social good, economic commodity — has meaning, and these meanings differ from society to society."[146] It is within this context that alcohol use in Ghana is being considered in this study.

The ritual use of alcohol within the African (Ghanaian) context is very crucial to the very pursuit of life since it serves as a bridge between the physical and spiritual worlds through libation.[147] Alcohol is considered as an indispensable fluid that opened doors spiritually and socially. It is viewed as possessing potent spiritual power without which communication is truncated with the spiritual or unseen world, through libation.

> The worldviews of the Akan, Ga-Adangme, and Ewe people of southern Ghana encompassed the living, the dead, and the unborn in a religious structure in which interaction with the Supreme Being, the ancestors, and the gods occupied a central place in day to day existence.

---

[144] See Boris Serebo. "Total Alcohol Consumption as an Index of Anxiety Among Urbanized Africans." *British Journal of Psychiatry* 67 (1972) p. 251-254. Also, Robin Room, "Alcohol Problems and the City," *British Journal of Addiction"* 85 (1990), p. 1395-1402.

[145] Akyeampong, *Drink, Power, and Cultural Change*, p. 2f.

[146] Akyeampong, p. 4; See also, Mary Douglas, ed. *Constructive Drinking Perspectives on Drink from Anthropology* (Cambridge, 1987).

[147] Libation is prayer accompanied and punctuated by the pouring of alcohol. It essentially involves three processes: invoking the presence of the Supreme Being, the gods and the ancestors; explaining to these supernatural beings the purpose and occasion for the human gathering; and supplicating these spirits to grant the human beings success in their endeavours. See Peter Sarpong, *Libation* (Accra: Anansesem Publications, 1996); Also, Marion Kilson, "Libation in Ga Ritual," *Journal of Religion in Africa* 2, 3 (1969) p. 161-178.

> Communication with the spiritual world was essential in
> the pursuit of social goals, and drink facilitated
> communication between the spiritual and physical world
> . . . Human subsistence and prosperity was predicated on
> a harmonious balance between the physical and spiritual
> realms.[148]

Due to its spiritual potency, alcohol is considered as a treasured fluid whose capacity to bridge the gap between the spiritual and physical worlds, so as to maintain a harmonious balance for human existence, cannot be exaggerated and its sacredness must be protected from abuse. However, according to Akyeampong, "the value of alcohol as an economic good and a social marker threatened its more sacred functions."[149] This culminated in efforts historically and socio-culturally to protect and restrict its use.

Alcohol is used to seal individual and communal transactions and also used in all forms of celebrations. According to Ghunney, alcohol serves as food in many African societies since some African alcoholic beers are made like porridge. Also, such drinks in Africa are mostly home-brewed and made from maize, sugarcane, millet, or sorghum.[150] Ghunney suggests that throughout the savannah belt of West Africa, almost all staple grains are fermented and cooked into beer and this is regarded as part of the daily diet. This also makes people drink since they see its nutritional value and conclude that it is okay to drink that type of alcohol. For Barbara Hagerman, all social gatherings have beer as the central element and "it is a source of much embarrassment for a household to receive a visitor and be unable to locate or buy the beer necessary for the expression of hospitality."[151]

The social context of alcohol cannot be under-estimated when reflecting on alcohol use and its effects on the African family. As noted, it plays a very important role in the communal and individual religious and socio-cultural purview of the

---

[148] Akyeampong, *Drink, Power, and Cultural Change*, p. 5.

[149] Akyeampong, *Drink, Power, and Cultural Change*, p. 21.

[150] Joseph Kow Ghunney. *Peer Counselling Manual: Life Skills Training for Young People*. New York: General Board of Global Missions, United Methodist Church, 2005, p. 48.

[151] B. L. Hagerman. "Food for Thought: Beer in a Social Ritual Context in West African Society," *Journal of Drug Issues,*18 4, 1980, p. 207.

African. Ceremonies such as naming, puberty rites, marriage, festivals, funerals, as well as communal activities such as fishing and farming, always see alcohol use being employed. In Ghana, traditional social and religious gatherings, as suggested earlier, start with the pouring of libation. During naming ceremonies, which come with the birth of a child, liquor as well as drops of water are put on the child's tongue to symbolize teaching the child to be able to distinguish between what is right and wrong. Marriages are sealed with the giving and sharing of a communal drink. In times of death and bereavement, alcohol features significantly in announcing the death and for receiving mourners. In some communities, mourners may not be permitted to eat but are allowed to use wine as food during such ceremonies. Libation is also poured during traditional transfer of land to seal the transaction and make it valid. Also, during processes of reconciliation, mediation and arbitration, alcohol is used and libation poured as a sign of resolution. In some societies, communal drinking is the norm and sometimes, people have to drink from the same glass or calabash as a sign of bonding.[152]

This does not mean that the African or the Ghanaian is a natural alcoholic because of the extensive use of alcohol in every situation. In other words, the fact that it is widely used does not mean the Ghanaian is ignorant of its hazardous effects. Although alcohol is central to all important rituals and ceremonies, "it was always public and communal and was circumscribed by rules and regulations."[153] An example is when it is used to teach a child moral lessons at *outdooring* ceremonies.[154] Drink is depicted as wrong and water as right.

Though it is believed to contain spiritual power and its place in the social and ritual order of the African cannot be negated, it is known that it could also dethrone reason due to its dangerous and ambiguous qualities. This capacity of alcohol is not unknown to the African. For Rattray, "no people in the world are more cognizant of the evils of alcoholic excess than the Ashanti."[155]

---

[152] Ghunney, *African Spiritual Worldview*, p. 42ff.

[153] Akyeampong, *Drink, Power, and Cultural Change*, p. 27.

[154] Outdooring ceremonies are occasions when the new-born child is brought outdoors and presented to the community (family and friends) at a public gathering. The ceremony usually takes place on the 8th or 15th day after the birth of the child, depending on the health of the child and the mother. It is mostly on this occasion that naming of the child also takes place.

Despite its prevalent use in the socio-cultural and religious order of the African or Ghanaian, African people or communities are still conversant with its disastrous effects on the individual as well as family and community and therefore frown on excessive, solitary drinking which often leads to such disastrous consequences. It is now very common to hear adults castigating young men for abusing alcohol. The context within which people understood the significance of alcohol and the social meanings attached to it is very significant for this study and is explored in the next section. The African context is one in which family relations is very much emphasized. One can see from the above, that one significant context in which the religio-socio-cultural use of alcohol is employed is the family setting. The family is therefore a central agency in alcohol use. As this study seeks to focus on alcoholism in the family, an explication of family systems theory is therefore very significant at this point to help us understand how the problem of an individual is best understood by considering its systemic affiliations.

Family Systems Thinking

Over the years, many theories of human behaviour have evolved. They have all sought to reflect on why human beings behave the way they do and how one can seek redemption for one's emotional and traumatic difficulties. Several of these theories have placed emphasis on the individual, especially with regard to the causes and purposes, as well as cognitive, emotional and behavioural processes involved in the individual's problems and coping. Freud's psychoanalytic theory with its several variations by Jung and Adler, and Carl Rogers' Person-centered Therapy, all belong to this category of individual therapy. One later development that "has to do with the way we order the world about us" is called *systems thinking*. This process shifts from the individual therapy and emphasizes that each component does not have its own discrete identity or input, but operates as part of a larger whole. According to Friedman, "the components do not function according to their 'nature' but according to their position in the network."[156] It is in this context that family systems thinking was developed, and served as a paradigm shift

---

[155] R.S. Rattray. *Ashanti* (Oxford, 1923) p. 135.
[156] Friedman, *Generation to Generation*, p. 15.

or a fourth force to psychodynamic, behavioural and humanistic/existentialist approaches to counselling and psychotherapy.

This view or approach holds that individuals are best understood through an assessment of the interactions within an entire family. Dysfunctional symptoms in an individual are often "viewed as an expression of a dysfunction within a family."[157] Such dysfunctional patterns are seen as being passed on through several generations. This approach, for Friedman, "focused on the overall relationship system of the family rather than psychodynamics of its members."[158] Hence, it differentiates *systems thinking* from the individual models. Is this to suggest that an individual's problems have more to do with the family's relational networks? Does this seek to de-emphasize the notion that our conflicts and anxieties are due primarily to the make-up of our personalities? Will this not seek to make people irres- ponsible for their actions and behaviours?

The one principal theme of all family therapy practitioners is that "the client is connected to living systems and that change in one part of the unit reverberates throughout other parts."[159] This is due to the fact that the family is seen as an *interactional unit*, with its own set of unique traits. Any approach to treatment must consider other family members and the larger context as well as the individual client. It will therefore be inaccurate to assess the concerns of an individual without observing the interaction of other family members, as well as the broader contexts in which the person and the family live. Within this framework, focus is on interpersonal dynamics rather than the internal dynamics of an individual. The family is viewed as a functioning unit that is more than the sum of the roles of its various members, and consequently "provides context for understanding how individuals function in relationship to others and how they behave."[160] Any action by an individual family member will invariably influence all other family members whose response will in turn have a reciprocal

---

[157] Gerald Cor *y*. *Theory and Practice of Counselling and Psychotherapy*. Fifth edition. Pa ific Grove, California: Brooks/Cole Publishing Company, 1996, p. 367.
[158] Friedman, *Generation to Generation*, p. 13.
[159] Corey, *Theory and Practice*, p. 367.
[160] Corey, *Theory and Practice*, p. 368.

effect on the individual. This process does not seek to de-emphasize the role of the individual in the family but rather to emphasize the fact that an individual's systemic affiliations and interactions have significant power in the person's life.[161] A change in an individual is accordingly facilitated by a change in the system. One's functionality is determined by the way the family is functioning. It is also a manifestation of the nature of interactions within the family system.

Friedman views the family as the true ecumenical experience of all humankind, and that its beliefs and practices are factors that contribute to our stress. He therefore suggests that one's ultimate functioning in real life depends on other "differentiating factors such as motivation and resiliency."[162] Thus, an entry into the multigenerational processes of families within a given culture gives one an unusual therapeutic potential. He writes:

> Ultimately, healing and survival depend on existential categories: on vision, for example, on hope, on the imaginative capacity, on the ability to transcend the anxiety of those about us, and on a response to challenge that treats crisis as opportunity for growth.[163]

Generally speaking, systemic thinking seeks to focus on the family relationships within which the continuation of one's problem "makes sense." It explores the system for family process and rules, perhaps using a genogram; concerned with transgenerational meanings, rules, cultural and gender perspectives within the system, community and larger systems affecting the family. Also, it seeks to intervene in ways designed to help change the context. Thus, the goal of family therapy is to seek "change in the system, which is assumed to produce change in the individual members."[164] This is to help family members change the dysfunctional patterns of relations and create functional ways of interacting. Though this process "may be slow, requiring patience, understanding, and often carefully planned

---

[161] Corey, *Theory and Practice*, p. 369.
[162] Friedman, *Generation to Generation*, p. 5.
[163] Friedman, *Generation to Generation*, p. 5.
[164] Corey, *Theory and Practice*, p. 368.

interventions," its success enables the family to learn about patterns that have been transmitted from generation to generation or learn ways to detect and solve problems that keep members stuck as dysfunctional individuals or in dysfunctional relational patterns.[165]

Several unresolved issues in families tend to manifest in individuals in so many ways, including alcoholism and it is for this reason that the family system must not be neglected in any therapeutic process. Bowen suggests that a family can best be understood when it is analyzed from at least a three-generation perspective, because a predictable pattern of interpersonal relationships connect the functioning of family members across generations. For there to be a great degree of wholeness or to achieve maturity as a unique personality, unresolved emotional fusion in one's family must be addressed. This is because "the cause of an individual's problems can be understood only by viewing the role of the family as an emotional unit."[166] Bowen therefore suggests a method for the organization of data, explanation of past events and the prediction of future events, so as to offer a "solid theoretical base" on which the therapeutic practice is built, thus making practices generally consistent.[167] These are reflected in the key concepts on which systemic thinking is applied.

Bowen identifies eight key concepts of family systems as: *differentiation of the self, triangulation, the nuclear family emotional system, the family-projection process, emotional cutoff, the multigenerational transmission process, sibling position* and *societal aggression.*[168] However, Friedman places them distinctly under five basic interrelated concepts. Taken together, they seek to "form a useful matrix for understanding the similarities and the crossovers" among families. These concepts, as elucidated by Friedman, and which the writer finds useful in this context, mark clearly the distinction between the family model and the individual models. [169] These are:

---

[165] Corey, *Theo y and Practice*, p. 368f.
[166] Corey, *The ry and Practice*, p. 371.
[167] See Murray Bowen. *Family Theory in Clinical Practice*. Northvale, New Jersey: Jason Aronson Inc., 1978.
[168] Corey, *Theory and Practice*, p. 374.
[169] Friedman, *Generation to Generation*, p. 19.

1. The Identified Patient.
2. Homeostasis (Balance).
3. Differentiation of the Self.
4. Extended Family Field.
5. Emotional Triangles.

The Identified Patient

By this concept, "the family member with the obvious symptom is to be seen not as the 'sick one' but as the one in whom the family's stress or pathology has surfaced."[170] This could manifest in a child as excessive bedwetting, hyperactivity, school failures, obesity, drugs, or juvenile diabetes. In a spouse, its form could be excessive drinking, depression, chronic ailments, a heart condition or perhaps even cancer. In an aged member of the family it could show up as confusion, senility, or agitated random behaviour.

This concept is used so as to avoid isolating the "problemed" family member from the overall relationship system of the family. Medically, it has been established that problems in any organ can be related to excessive over-functioning, under-functioning or dysfunction of another. Thus, the *identified patient*, just like the defective organ, must not be treated in isolation. Friedman suggests that in family theory, where the organism is the human family, "when one part of that organism is treated in isolation from its interconnections with another, as though the problem were solely its own, fundamental change is not likely."[171] What rather happens is that the symptom tends to recycle, either in the same or different form, or in the same or different member. Thus, any attempt to "cure" a person in isolation from his or her family, says family theory, is as misdirected, and ultimately ineffective, as transplanting a healthy organ into a body whose unbalanced chemistry will destroy the new one as it did the old.[172] Biblically, it is like "putting new wine into old wineskins." By keeping the focus on one of its members, the family can deny the very issues that contributed to make one of its members symptomatic, even if it ultimately harms the entire family.

---

[170] Friedman, *Generation to Generation*, p. 19.
[171] Friedman, *Generation to Generation*, p. 19f.
[172] Friedman, *Generation to Generation*, p. 20.

Homeostasis (Balance)

With family system processes, the problem of a family lies in the nature of the system rather than in the nature of its component parts. The concept of homeostasis, for Friedman, emphasizes "the tendency of any set of relationships to strive perpetually, in self-corrective ways, to preserve the organizing principles of its existence."[173] This suggests that no matter what the "quirks or idiosyncrasies" of the various members are, for the system to exist and have a name, it ought to have achieved some kind of balance in order to permit the continuity necessary for maintaining its identity.

Using an illustration of a thermostat, Friedman suggests that this concept is not static but a dynamic one as when a thermostat controls the temperature balance, not at a fixed point, but within a range. Families are a mutually causative system, whose complementary behaviour reinforces and perpetuates the nature of their interactions. In general systems theory, this concept of homeostasis or self-regulating behaviour is aimed at maintaining balance as thermostatically controlled equipment. Here, behaviours are seen as a series of moves and countermoves in a repeating cycle so as to maintain balance. This process of cause and effect is generally referred to as circular causality. In this case, the one who started the sequence is not considered relevant for resolving it, because once underway, these sequences seem to be self-perpetuating.[174] "Similarly, the fact that the balance in a family system has gone beyond the range of its own thermostat is not always bad."[175] Change is therefore necessary. This helps explain why a given relationship or family becomes troubled, by shedding light on which family member becomes, or is likely to become symptomatic (the identified patient). It illuminates the family's resistance to change and assists in creating strategies for change, and also, "help develop

---

[173] Friedman, *Generation to Generation*, p. 23.

[174] Michael P. Nichols. *Family Therapy: Concepts and Methods* (Needham Heights, MA.: Allyn and Bacon, 1984) pp. 129-131. See also, Carolyn J. Bohler, "Essential Elements of Family Systems Approaches to Pastoral Counselling" in *Clinical Handbook of Pastoral Counselling*, Volume 1, Expanded Edition. Eds. Robert Wicks, Richard Parsons and Donald Capps, Mahway: NJ.: Paulist Press, 1993, pp. 585-613.

[175] Friedman, *Generation to Generation*, p. 24.

criteria for distinguishing real change from the recycling of a symptom."[176]

Differentiation of the Self

This is one of the most important concepts in the whole theory. According to Murray Bowen "the one most important goal of family systems therapy is to help family members toward a better level of 'differentiation of self.'"[177] Bowen suggests that the differentiation of self-scale on a simple level conveys "that people are basically different from each other and it is possible to classify them according to these differences."[178] This hypothesis of a scale of differentiation is to suggest its meaning.

> Differentiation means the capacity of a family member to define his or her own life's goals and values apart from surrounding togetherness pressures; to say "I" when others are demanding "you" and "we". It includes the capacity to maintain a (relatively) non-anxious presence in the midst of anxious systems, to take maximum responsibility for one's own destiny or emotional being. It can be measured somewhat by the breadth of one's repertoire of responses when confronted with crisis . . . Differentiation means the capacity to be an "I" while remaining connected.[179]

Families and other social groups tremendously affect how people think, feel and act, but individuals vary in susceptibility to a "group think" and groups vary in the amount of pressure they exert for conformity. The differences between individuals and between groups reflect differences in people's levels of differentiation. The less developed a person's self, the more impact others have on his functioning and the more he tries to control, actively or passively, the functioning of others. Bowen suggests that the basic building blocks of a self are inborn. The individual's family relationships during childbirth and adolescence, primarily determine how much the "self" develops. Once established, the level of self rarely changes unless a person makes a structured

[176] Friedman, *Generation to Generation*, p. 24.
[177] Bowen, *Family Therapy in Clinical Practice*, p. 529.
[178] Bowen, *Family Therapy*, p. 534.
[179] Friedman, *Generation to Generation*, p. 27.

and intentional effort to change it. Thus, differentiation of the self, "involves both the psychological separation of intellect and emotion and independence of the self from others."[180] Individuals who are differentiated are able to choose between being guided by their feelings and by their thoughts.

People who are undifferentiated, generally, have difficulty in separating themselves from others and tend to fuse with dominant emotional patterns in the family. Such people tend to depend heavily on the acceptance and approval of others to the extent that they are quick to adjust what they think, say, and do to please others. They have a low "degree of autonomy, react emotionally" and are "unable to take a position on issues."[181] On the other hand, a well-differentiated person tends to recognize one's realistic dependence on others, but still can stay clear headed enough in the face of conflict, criticism, and rejection; to distinguish thinking rooted in a careful assessment of the facts from thinking clouded by emotions. Thoughtfully acquired principles help guide decision-making about important family and social issues, putting one less at the mercy of the feelings of the moment. This is what Friedman means when he emphasizes maintaining a "non-anxious presence."[182] Basically, this concept seeks to suggest that every human society, on a scale of differentiation will have its well-differentiated people, poorly differentiated people and people who are between these two extremes. Thus, the levels of differentiation of family members consequently determine the levels of their emotional interdependence. This also emphasizes the fact that one does not have to "blame forces outside the family for problems inside the family."[183] The essence of self-differentiation is the ability of maintaining a non-anxious presence in the midst of an anxious system; being a part of, yet separated from the system.

Family of Origin (Extended Family Field)

Closely related to the concept of self-differentiation is the concept of family of origin. This family of origin refers to one's nuclear and extended family. In family systems thinking, the entire

---

[180] Corey, *Theory and Practice*, p. 374.
[181] Corey, *Theory and Practice*.
[182] Friedman, *Generation to Generation*, p. 30.
[183] Friedman, *Generation to Generation*.

network of family system is very important and its influence over generations is very significant. According to Friedman, "gaining a better understanding of the emotional processes still at work with regard to our family of origin, and modifying our response to them, can aid significantly in the resolution of emotional problems in our immediate family."[184] This concept emphasizes that family issues are passed on from generation to generation. Specific behaviour patterns, perceptions, and thinking, as well as specific issues, such as sex, money, territory, drinking, separation, and health, have an "uncanny way of reappearing."[185] Family members must therefore see beyond the horizons of their own nuclear family area of trouble and observe the transmission of such issues. This enables them to obtain more distance from their immediate problems and as a result, become free to make changes.

The extended family field plays a very important role in one's process of differentiation. One's position in the family of origin is the source of one's uniqueness, the basic parameter for one's emotional potential as well as one's difficulties. This unique position that can dictate or nourish one's natural strengths is the only thing one cannot share or give to another as long as one is still alive. Thus, the more one understands that position and the more we can learn to occupy it with grace and 'savvy' rather than fleeing from it or unwittingly allowing it to programme our destiny, the more effectively we can function in any other area of our life.[186]

If differentiation of the self is a process in which an individual acquires a sense of "self identity," then "differentiation from the family of origin enables one to accept personal responsibility for one's thoughts, feelings, perceptions, and actions."[187] This process of differentiation, *individuation*, is not simply physically leaving one's family of origin. It is not a "fixed destination" that has to be reached once and for all but rather, it is a life-long developmental process that is achieved relative to the family of origin.[188] As one becomes aware of the power of the extended family, one is able to take responsibility for oneself

---

[184] Friedman, *Generation to Generation*, p. 31.
[185] Friedman, *Generation to Generation*.
[186] Friedman, *Generation to Generation*, p. 34.
[187] Corey, *Theory and Practice*, p. 374.
[188] Corey, *Theory and Practice*.

and make contributions that will seek to enhance his/her relationships. Hence one's coping mechanism in handling crises, in whatever way, is enhanced. Inability to properly differentiate from one's family of origin causes parents to project their unconscious fears and feelings of inadequacy unto their children. Children therefore tend to inherit such problems while tending to blame oneself for the happiness of the other.

Triangulation (Emotional Triangles)

Significant in Bowen's multigenerational model is triangulation which offers a way of putting into operation the previous four concepts in counselling and psychotherapy. Within intimate relationships, anxiety is prone to develop. "Under stressful situations, two people may recruit a third person into the relationship to reduce the anxiety and gain stability. This is called triangulation."[189] Though triangulation lessens the emotional tension between two people, it does not address the underlying conflict, but worsens the situation in the long run. A couple with an unresolved problem and intense conflict may tend to focus their attention on a problematic son instead of dealing with each other. Their basic problem remains unsolved and once the son is no longer around or leaves home, the problem rears its "ugly head" and they often resume fighting, which may lead to divorce. Thus, one is said to be "triangled" when he/she gets caught in the middle as the focus of such unresolved issue.

> When any two parts of a system becomes uncomfortable with another, they will "triangle in" or focus upon a third person, or issue, as a way of stabilizing their own relationship with one another.[190]

Generally, the focus of emotional triangle is on "process rather than content" and provides one with a new way of hearing people as well as criteria for what information is important. It is commonly said, "What Peter says to you about Paul tells you more about Peter than it does about Paul." However, in the concept of emotional triangle, "What Peter says to you about his relationship with Paul has to do with his relationship with

---

[189] Corey, *Theory and Practice.*
[190] Friedman, *Generation to Generation*, p. 35.

you."[191] Though there are several ways of triangulation, maintaining a non-anxious presence and not distancing oneself is extremely significant. This is because distancing oneself ultimately preserves the triangle. Friedman thus surmises that "the most triangulated person in any set of relationships is always the most vulnerable." The laws of emotional triangles tend to become the most powerful, when well understood.[192]

To further elucidate and offer more insights so as to enable one think more deeply about alcoholism in terms of family processes, Friedman describes ten "*laws*" of family life derived from family theory. He enumerates these as *emotional distance, loss and replacement, chronic conditions, pain and responsibility, the paradox of seriousness and the seriousness of paradox, secrets and systems, sibling position, diagnosis, symmetry,* and *survival in families.* According to him, thinking in terms of family process involves more than the application of new ideas. "It represents a shift in paradigms, a change in the very manner of conceptualizing emotional phenomena."[193] These laws seek to get one acquainted and accustomed to family system theory and is thus an "effort to demythologize several assumptions about family life that have resulted from an effort to conceptualize families as the interactions of individuals rather than individuals as the components of families."[194] All this emphasizes the fact that all individuals are interconnected so that a change in one person affects other family members, while at the same time the other family members have an effect on that person's behaviours, thoughts and feelings.[195] To therefore understand the individual's symptomatic behaviour and to bring meaningful restoration in this case, the family must be considered as a unit in understanding the problem and in restoring the system to normalcy.

Alcoholism and the Family System

One can critically deduce from the above conception of family systems theory that since families could be healthy or unhealthy,

---

[191] Friedman, *Generation to Generation.*
[192] Friedman, *Generation to Generation*, ff.
[193] Friedman, *Generation to Generation*, p. 40.
[194] Friedman, *Generation to Generation.*
[195] Bohler, *Essential Elements*, p. 587.

and in view of the fact that alcoholism destroys the normal functioning of an individual (*the identified patient*) within the family, the concept of alcoholism as a family disease invariably renders the family unhealthy or dysfunctional. Also, the hereditary and genetic nature of alcoholism as a disease makes it a multigenerational ailment, the treatment of which must consider the entire system by focusing on any family of origin issues.

The effect of alcoholism on families, as proposed earlier, varies, depending on the nature and the dynamics of the family system itself. This makes every family have its own story to tell. Spickard and Thompson assert that "whatever personality differences exist among alcoholics, their family members frequently react in predictable ways to the strain of living with an addict."[196] These reactions, accordingly "can become as obsessive and compulsive as the alcoholic's own behaviour, and as such, they often threaten to leave family members clinically sicker than the alcoholic."[197] According to Royce, families have their own ways of denying the problem. They have developed their own homeostatic adjustment to the drinking, to the extent of reversing roles. Also, "some family members get adjusted to an alcoholic environment that they think it is normal and cannot live out their proper roles in sobriety."[198] This seeks to explain why many daughters of alcoholic fathers end up marrying an alcoholic. Royce quotes one such daughter as saying defensively, "I know what buttons to push." This is a very clear example of what is meant by the whole family is sick. Whether the alcoholic or the acting out juvenile delinquent or the nagging wife, it is very important to stop using one person as a scapegoat (identified patient).[199]

Central to this theme of family systems is the belief that changes in any part of the system (any family member) affects all the others who also in response make changes in an attempt to maintain family cohesion or equilibrium. According to Jean Kinney, family members have different approaches to living with an alcoholic, which are all used at various times. For Kinney, there are three approaches: (i) Keeping out of the way of the

---

[196] Spickard and Thompson, *Dying for a Drink*, p. 68.

[197] Spickard and Thompson, *Dying for a Drink*.

[198] Royce, *Alcohol and Other Drug Dependencies*, p. 517.

[199] Royce, *Alcohol and Other Drug Dependencies*.

drinker and managing one's own life; (ii) care giving, counselling, and controlling; and (iii) resigning and maintaining a façade. The use of such approaches, however, differs among men and women.[200] To better understand how families are affected as they strive to maintain homeostasis, an explication of the term, *codependency* cannot be avoided in reflecting on alcoholism and the family system.

Codependency

The concept of codependency seeks to emphasize how family members, those affected, can become as sick as those afflicted because they try to control the drinking as their lives are built around the one drinking. For Clinebell,"they organize their lives around 'helping' the addicted by attempting to control them, protecting them from the painful consequences of their actions, and taking responsibility for their destructive behaviour."[201] Thus, "codependents are obsessively dependent on the dependence of addicted members to maintain a sense of their own security, power, and self-esteem."[202] This we can conclude is an unhealthy relationship that must be responsibly curtailed so as to foster growth in the family. Albers defines codependency as:

> A primary lifestyle disorder occasioned by adaptation to and being enmeshed with an unhealthy relationship or relationships which result in the loss of a person's sense of self or a group's sense of identity. As family members have adjusted, readjusted, and finally maladjusted to the dysfunctional situation, codependency occurs.[203]

For Albers, however, codependency does not just occur in individual family members' relationships with the addicted one and in the collective interaction of their family system, but also in congregations as social systems of shared faith.[204] Codepen-

---

[200] Kinney, *Loosening the Grip*, p. 202f.

[201] Clinebell, *Understanding and Counselling* p. 26.

[202] Clinebell, *Understanding and Counselling*.

[203] Robert H. Albers. "Codependency: Characteristic or Caricature?" *Journal of Ministry in Addiction and Recovery* 2, no. 1 (1995): p.1-2 as quoted in Clinebell, p. 403.

[204] Albers, *Codependency*, p. 403.

dency is therefore not an abstract term but one that clearly suggests that family members become as sick as the individual alcoholic as they strive to maintain the family's sense of identity. According to Clinebell, there are some hidden dynamics in codependency which Charlotte Davis Kasl, a psychologist, succinctly illuminates.

> The goal of codependent behaviour is to find externally the security and power that is lacking internally. The belief system is that one cannot exist on one's own, and one therefore must do whatever it takes to keep a partner and any other symbols of security, such as home, children, and financial support.[205]

This process according to Clinebell has psychological as well as theological implications. Psychologically, those who are addicted to codependency are caught on a nonstop treadmill trying in vain to earn their acceptance by taking care of others. Theologically, it is a graceless attempt to earn their salvation by their good works.[206]

Closely linked to this concept of codependency is *enabling*. This describes the behaviour of codependent family members, friends, employers, or helping professionals, including clergy, who unwittingly enable addicted persons to continue their self-other damaging behaviour which invariably includes futile, frustrating efforts to control the addicted person's drinking or drug use.[207] For Kinney, enabling occurs whenever "the family's actions protect the alcohol dependent member from the consequences of drinking." Though this is aimed at relieving their own pain and in an attempt to live with and around the illness, "the family's behaviour often unwittingly allows the drinking to continue."[208]

Ironically, while sparing the alcohol-dependent person from experiencing the consequences and thus the associated

---

[205] Charlotte Davis Kasl. *Many Roads, One Journey: Moving Beyond the Twelve Steps.* New York: Harper Collins, 1992, p. 266 as quted in Clinebell, *Understanding and Counselling*, p. 403.

[206] Clinebell, *Understanding and Counselling*, p. 403.

[207] Clinebell, *Understanding and Counselling*, p. 26f.

[208] Kinney, *Loosening the Grip*, p. 200.

pain, the family members absorb the pain themselves . . . Enabling behaviours can evoke twinges of guilt, anger, despair, frustration, and shame. To draw upon a metaphor from a family systems approach commonly used in psychotherapy, the enabler and alcoholic are in "escalating equilibrium." This means that the behaviour of each reinforces and maintains the other, while also raising the costs and emotional consequences for both.[209]

Thus, the family invariably takes away the impetus for change through enabling behaviours that tend to remove costs that result from drinking.

Consequently, whatever module of recovery is proposed for the alcoholic, there must be a process of recovery for the family as well so as not to keep the family perpetually dysfunctional or unable to overcome the powerful impact of alcoholism in the family. This is because as the individual becomes powerless over his addiction, the family is also rendered powerless by the helplessness of the addict. For this reason, struggle for survival becomes sets of defence mechanisms that are entangled in unrealistic disparaging behaviours. Dysfunctional or unhealthy families of alcoholics often grapple with feelings of shame, guilt, fear, anger, emptiness, loneliness, helplessness, hopelessness, depression, sadness, and worthlessness — however, rarely are any of these feelings, including positive ones, expressed appropriately.

Generally, children receive messages about their worth from their parents, grandparents, siblings, family, teachers, friends and community members. They learn from experience and by visual perception. In a research analysis by Bloom, he suggested that fifty percent of the child's intelligence is developed in the first four years of life, twenty percent from age four to eight, and twenty percent from ages eight to seventeen. This shows that the ages which the child spends with parents, building trust-mistrust, influence one's development more.

There are thirteen factors that influence the growth of intelligence. All of these factors are related to the family, such as the intellectual aspirations the parents have for

---

[209] Kinney, *Loosening the Grip*, p. 203f.

the child, the rewards they offer for mental achievement, the opportunities for learning that are provided, the guidance they offer to make ordinary events educational, and the general situation in the house that encourages the proper use of language. [210]

This suggests that the provision of an apt environment for the appropriate nurturing of a child is a key responsibility of the family since family experiences "often set the tone for later expectations, aspirations or ambitions, traditions as well as religious and moral beliefs and attitudes."[211] A dysfunctional family will therefore invariably produce a dysfunctional child given that the family is the strongest agent of reinforcement of traditions, practices, morals, faith, and beliefs. Consequently, when feelings of pain and problems are being sedated with alcohol, it tends to be emulated as a lifestyle by those growing up in such an environment, a lifestyle to be perpetuated from generation to generation. Thus, families that are experiencing a great deal of pain over a period of time, who are entangled in a conspiracy of silence and its gradations and overwhelming derivations, are unable to nurture the feeling of self-worth of each family member and hence not able to maintain homeostasis.[212] In this situation, whatever pain is being experienced begets more pain, resulting in chaos and instability. Participants in the system thereby tend to develop strategies and coping mechanisms to cover up the resultant chaos and confusion. "The apparent arrogance we see is probably denial and an attempt to cope with their sense of helplessness," which oftentimes takes the form of projections on others.[213] Such defence mechanisms tend to perpetuate the addiction process and the concomitant results of this dysfunctionality are predictable. Thus, the whole system needs to get some attention and treatment by adapting to any shift or change in its

---

[210] C. Ellis Nelson. Ed. Issues Facing Christian Educators Today: *A Report Based on the World Institute on Christian Education Meeting in Nairobi, Kenya.* World Council on Christian Education: July, 1967, p. 27f.

[211] Mary A. Love. *Potpourri for Christian Educators*, revised edition (Charlotte, N.C.: A.M.E. Zion Publishing House, 1988) p. 60.

[212] *The Awakening, Treatment Manual*, Week 6 p. 4.

[213] Royce, *Alcohol and Other Drug Dependencies*, p. 510.

equilibrium. "The homeostatic principle is operative and unless there is systemic change, individual change within the system is difficult."[214] The relevance of this theory in the pursuit of wholeness cannot be denied in the African context due essentially to the relational and communal nature of the African way of life.

As noted, the family as a system is made up of component parts that are linked together in a certain way to accomplish a common purpose. Thus, be it one parent, two parents, nuclear or extended family, children or no children, each member of the family has a specific role to play to keep the system together. An alcoholic family becomes more dysfunctional when there is a loss of one or more of the family members through death, separation, illness or side effects of alcoholism; or through emotional loss such as withdrawal, anger and abuse.[215] Such physical or emotional loss as well as the threat of such loss is very real to family members. In Ghana as well as other developing countries, for example, the experience of severe trauma through human experience of suffering, the reality of political unrest, pervasive poverty, unemployment, prospect of starvation, rape and defilement, and the pervading sense of hopelessness and helplessness in the face of these grim realities, from the time one is an infant, somehow creates a hotbed for addiction which invariably confronts one with the reality and power of death.[216] This does not mean that the alcoholic and his/her family have no quest for survival or for finding meaning in life.

In an alcoholic family, there is a common purpose for survival. While the individual alcoholic person's goal is to use drink, the family tends to become obsessed with the alcoholic's behaviour in relation to drinking. This renders the family's desire of working towards survival to be curtailed since it cannot maintain its balance. The entire family is now confronted with trying to cope with the bizarre and manipulative behaviour of the alcoholic, while maneuvering itself through the traumatic stresses and crises of the situation. Such beleaguering stresses and traumas of alcoholism certainly cause those affected to seek

---

[214] Robert H. Albers, "The Search for Meaning," *Journal of Ministry in Addiction and Recovery*, Vol. 6 (2) 1999. The Haworth Press Inc, 1999, p. 3f.

[215] *The Awakening, Treatment Manual*, Week 6 p. 4.

[216] Albers, *The Search for Meaning*, p. 1-9.

meaning in life through meaningful relationships and interactions. This results in the quest for a spirituality that will help in quenching the addictive thirst that plagues those beleaguered with addiction, thereby connecting their experiences and reflections upon their own suffering.

An Exploration of Health and Wholeness

Wholeness is an indispensable and much sought after aspect of life and can be described in different ways by different people. In this context, it seeks to suggest wellness or the totality of one's being in relation to community — the total well-being of a person in all its dimensions. To be whole does not only mean the absence of diseases, but to be in good health. According to the World Health Organization (WHO), health is a "state of complete physical, mental and social well-being, and not merely the absence of infirmity."[217] This definition however falls short of considering the spiritual well-being which cannot be dismissed in the African context. In the African context the spiritual and relational dimension of one's personality cannot be relegated to the background. Wholeness in this context can therefore be described as the totality of one's well-being physically, mentally, socially and spiritually. Such a state of well-being in its totality is reflected in the Hebrew and biblical concept of *shalom*.

Though all expeditiously pursue wholeness, it is not easily attained. Wholeness is tantamount to being in good health. For Steinke, "health is wholeness." He suggests that to be healthy means having all parts of the human component working together to maintain balance.[218] This balance is, however, not static but dynamic since there is significant interplay of forces that influence one's pursuit for good health or wholeness. Andrew Igenoza suggests that "wholeness has to do with healing; the total well-being of a person or his or her total restoration in all its dimensions."[219] It is therefore not limited to

---

[217] "The Preamble to the Charter of the World Health Organization." See, *Encyclopedia Britannica*. Vol. 8, p. 68.

[218] Peter L Steinke. *Healthy Congregations: A Systems Approach*. The Alban Institute, 1996, p. vi.

[219] Andrew Olu Igenoza. "Wholeness in African Experience, Christian Perspectives," in *The Church and Healing- Echoes from Africa*, Emmanuel Lartey, Daisy Nwachuku, Kasonga Wa Kasonga (Eds.) Frankfurt am Main: Peter Lang, 1994, p. 126.

the physical well-being but also the emotional, psycho-social and spiritual well-being, not only of the individual but of the entire system of which the individual is a part. Due to its pervasive nature, alcoholism can therefore not be considered in relation to the individual's physiological and psycho-social relief only but also in spiritual restoration, not only the individual in isolation, but also in the family and the community of which the individual is a part.

Though wholeness could be considered differently by different people, for the African, the spiritual dimension to health cannot be overlooked since it is what essentially defines the personality of the individual in relation to community. The outlook of the African is fundamentally religious. African ontology is fundamentally spiritual and this invariably is intricately interwoven with its social, economic, political and religious organizations. For Lartey, "religion is pervasive in Ghana. It is a regular accompaniment in almost everyone's life."[220] For this reason, Joseph Ghunney contends that for the African, "when one loses one's spirituality, one loses one's personality."[221] One can therefore not live a meaningful life outside the context of the religious worldview of the community to which one belongs.

In this study, the view taken in considering wholeness is that of the Jewish concept of *shalom*. This is because *shalom* reflects God's vision for humankind and incorporates the physical and spiritual dimension of both individuals and the environment to which he or she belongs. It portrays a wholeness that encapsulates God's reconciling love, justice, redemption, liberation, truthfulness, and compassion. Jack Stotts in *Shalom: The Content of a Peaceful City*, asserts that one constant and pervasive symbol in Old Testament literature used for indicating the relationship that God establishes and intends for humankind and nature is *shalom*, which is often ordinarily translated as *peace*. In biblical texts, however, it (*shalom*) represents a broad range of meanings.

---

[220] Emmanuel Lartey. "Some Contextual Implications for Pastoral Counselling in Ghana," in *Pastoral Care and Counselling in Africa Today*, Jean Masamba ma Mpolo, Daisy Nwachuku, (Eds.) Frankfurt am Main: Peter Lang, 1991, p. 38.

[221] Joseph Kow Ghunney. *Lecture on African Christian Spirituality and Pastoral Care*, Trinity Theological Seminary, March 2006.

The core meaning is that of wholeness, health and security. Wholeness, health, and security do not mean individual tranquility in the midst of external turbulence. *Shalom* is not peace of mind, escape from the frustrations and care of the surrounding environment. Rather, *shalom* is a particular state of social existence. It is a state of existence where the claims and needs of all that are satisfied; where there is a relationship of communion between God and humans and nature, where there is fulfillment for all creation.[222]

This is a divine gift and does not arise out of human capabilities. As an ultimate gift, it may seem to be beyond human attainment, but the fact that we are incapable of *shalom* does not mean we do not aim for *shalom*. With every privilege comes a responsibility. In aiming at *shalom*, it therefore behoves all to affirm behaviours of respectfulness, assertiveness, accountability, and the inclusion of the larger common good (of the system) must serve as the standard.

We can herein surmise that *shalom* fundamentally means "totality," wholeness or wellness in its totality. According to Lartey, it "denotes not a state but a relationship of unity, solidarity, harmonious community, the exercise of mutual responsibility and confidence, the fulfilling of obligations and participation in community."[223] For Lartey, it also includes salvation, not only in the sense of deliverance from evil and other spiritual forces, but "wholeness," well-being and growth. This view is reflected in the general holistic conception of illness within the African context. According to Archbishop Emmanuel Milingo, healing can be defined as:

> Taking away from a person a disturbance in life which acts as a deprivation of self-fulfillment and which is considered an unwanted parasite. In whatever way we take it, the expected result is to release someone from a stumbling block to human fulfillment . . . So to heal in our [African] context, means to heal the whole person.[224]

---

[222] Jack L. Stotts. *Shalom: The Content of the Peaceful City.* Nashville, TN: Abingdon Press, 1973, p. 98.

[223] Lartey, *Some Contextual Implications*, p. 40.

[224] Emmanuel Milingo. *The World in Between: Christian Healing and the Struggle for Spiritual Survival.* London: C. Hurst and Co., 1984, p. 24, 25.

The Yoruba word, *Alafia*, for instance, translates as "health" but embraces much more than the physical. *Alafia* encapsulates "the totality of an individual's physical, social, psychological and spiritual well-being in his total environment settings."[225] As we have sought to emphasize, sickness in the African context connotes the absence of health as well as personal and relational well-being.[226] This condition of health in the African context, which is synonymous with the Hebrew *shalom*, is what we seek to emphasize in this book.

In this regard, therefore, pastoral encounters must move beyond individualistic and private understanding of human problems to incorporate an integral whole of cosmic and social events. Thus, with a breach in moral codes, the cosmic ties between one's self and the community are broken. To this end, a quest for wholeness must focus not only on the person to be cured, but broken ties and relationships that need to be restored. Thus, relationships must become whole. According to Abraham Berinyuu,

> Africans are convinced that in the activities of life, harmony, balance or tranquility must constantly be sought and maintained. Society is not segmented into, for example, medicine, sociology, law, politics and religion. Life is a liturgy of celebration for the victories and/or sacrifices of others.'[227]

This is more so because in this milieu, there is no differentiation between animate and inanimate, between spirit and matter, between living and non-living, physical and metaphysical, secular and sacred. It is believed that everything, including human beings, is in constant relationship with the cosmos and

---

[225] Godwin S. Soglo. "The Concept of Cause in African Thought," in *The African Philosophy Reader* (ed.) P.H. Coetzee and A.P.J. Roux. London and NY, 1998, p. 181.

[226] See Kwabena Asamoah-Gyadu. "Rethinking African Worldview of Mystical Causality: Mission and Ecclesiology in the Era of HIV/AIDS." Paper presented at the World Association for Christian Communication/ Trinity Theological Seminary Conference on 'Religion, Media and Health in West Africa' with a focus on HIV/AIDS at GIMPA, Accra, Ghana: December 13-15, 2006.

[227] A.A. Berinyuu. *Pastoral Care to the Sick in Africa: An Approach to Trans-cultural Pastoral Theology.* Frankfurt: Peter Lang, 1988, p. 5.

people are in constant relationship with such unseen forces and beings.[228] Thus, to be restored to wholeness or good health, according to Masamba ma Mpolo, involves:

> The restoration of broken relationships, the re-establishment of social equilibrium, the re-vitalization of individual identity within the context of the renewed community are all major means and dynamic ends underlying traditional therapies and healing processes.[229]

It is within this context and background that we consider the quest for wholeness as aimed at restoration of imbalance and harmony within and between persons and also with the unseen world. Such harmony is not only between persons in isolation, but persons in relationship and within the larger context of what makes a person "a human being." This is what spirituality, as we will see later, seeks to suggest. We will therefore proceed to do a meaningful reflection on what spirituality is and what it means for the alcoholic and his or her family in their quest for *shalom*.

Spirituality and Recovery

The goal of this study is not to reflect on the bio-medical and physical recovery programme for the alcoholic since this clearly falls within the purview of the bio-medical profession. However, several modules of recovery that have been reviewed earlier in this book seem to suggest that the most comprehensive treatment or recovery programme for the alcoholic are those that have sought to meet spiritual needs; making alcoholics admit their powerlessness over alcohol and recognizing the need to embrace a power greater than themselves. In doing so, they ought to embrace a harmonious relationship with the cosmos and fellow persons. Albers, Clinebell and Keller, have constantly suggested in many forms that the twelve-step programmes,[230] which involve one's admission of powerlessness over addiction and

---

[228] Berinyuu, *Pastoral Care*, p. 5.

[229] Masamba ma Mpolo. "Perspectives on African Pastoral Counselling," in *The Risks of Growth*, p. 10.

[230] For a more comprehensive work on 12-step programmes, see *Alcoholics Anonymous (The Big Book)* Third edition. A. A. World Services, Inc. 1976.

turning over oneself unto an Ultimate Reality (God), embraces a deep sense of spirituality and a communal sense of purpose. This concept seeks to emphasize spirituality as the central turning point in any recovery programme.

Albers notes that "the spiritual climate of the twelve step program is the key to its effective operation resulting in lives that are restored to wholeness and health." A close observation of these groups suggests that the key to recovery does not lie in their structure or organization, but "the centrality of a power greater than self stands at the heart of the movement."[231] Also, these programmes are communal in nature and not individualistic. "The spirituality of recovery is always bathed in the mutuality of the community."[232] Relationship with the transcendent and with humans is acknowledged as a source of strength on the way to sobriety as one endeavours to recapture meaning and purpose in life, in one's attempt to get out of the abyss of the despair and darkness which alcoholism has left one in. This situation invariably reverberates through the affected family as well. This calls for a more meaningful reflection on what spirituality entails and its implications for alcoholics and their families in the African Christian milieu.

Though the individual alcoholic's goal is to use alcohol, it certainly does not mean that he/she has no quest for survival. For Albers, the individual's quest for meaning in life comes to expression in questions such as "Why quit if there is no meaning in life?" "Why should I not get high if there is nothing else left in life?" "Why should I care about you or about me; isn't life just one damn thing after another anyway?" "Why should I change my lifestyle if I am not sure there is something better?" Such existential questions come from the depths of people who often are incredibly intelligent, sensitive and creative, and are repeatedly a result of a "deep inner spiritual quest for meaning in the light of existential realities that are beyond human comprehension."[233] This is certainly a search for continued existence. Such a search for meaning in life and for survival suggests that it will not be erroneous to affirm centrality of

---

[231] Robert H. Albers. "The Spirit and Spirituality of Twelve Step Groups," *Journal of Ministry in Addiction and Recovery*, Vol. 6, 1 (1999), p.4.

[232] Albers, "The Spirit and Spirituality," p. 6.

[233] Albers, "The Spirit and Spirituality," p. 2.

spirituality in the continuum of care for those affected as well as its necessity for those afflicted. We will therefore proceed to make a case for spirituality, as we explore the concept of wholeness, and its essential nature for those afflicted and affected in order to restore the system to a dynamic balance.

A meaningful reflection calls for an exposition of what generally characterizes spirituality. It also seeks to glance at spirituality in relation to religion. Some have sought to suggest that spirituality and religion are incompatible and that there exists an adversarial relationship between the two. "They are depicted as being antithetical to one another, the result of which often deteriorates into acrimony."[234] For this reason, the proponents of this position suggest that it is difficult to embrace both simultaneously. However, what is more significant is that in both contexts, there is a divine-human encounter and relationships are enhanced. In relation to addiction and recovery, wherever healing and health occur, wherever people are bonded together in constructive relationships, wherever relationships are established that encourage trust and honesty, wherever freedom from bondage is experienced, wherever the future is envisioned as a lure to a full and abundant life of joy and peace, God is at work among humankind, be it in the context of spirituality or religion. It will therefore be erroneous to suggest that spirituality and religion are adversaries. They should rather be seen as allies and mediums that God uses to provide restoration and wholeness to humankind.[235] Traditional African Religion, which is considered later in this study, significantly reveals that with religion and spirituality, as with the mundane and the holy, one cannot be considered aside from the other. It has been rightly acknowledged that healing in the context of African spirituality "incorporates all dimensions of human and cosmic life."[236] It is therefore an embodiment of the totality of the human personality in relation to community and to the

---

[234] Robert H Albers. "Spirituality and Religion: Allies or Adversaries?" *Journal of Ministry in Addiction and Recovery*, Vol. 4, 2 (1997) p. 1.

[235] Albers, "Spirituality and Religion," p. 1-8.

[236] Jean Masamba ma Mpolo. "Spirituality and Counselling for Healing and Liberation: The Context and Praxis of African Pastoral Activity and Psychotherapy." In *The Church and Healing: Echoes from Africa.* Emmanuel Lartey, Daisy Nwachuku, and Kasonga Wa Kasonga (Eds.), Frankfurt: Peter Lang, 1994, p. 16.

cosmos. It is in fulfillment of this goal that *shalom*, wholeness, is relevant.

Spirituality in Context

Spirituality has been variously conceptualized, depending on one's cultural heritage or tradition. It is, however, complex to define and its meaning is often vague. It is vague because if spirit is assumed to be the opposite of matter, spirituality then tends to be associated with the invisible. It is also distorted given that its meaning is often limited to spiritual disciplines such as prayer, fasting and meditation. Will this then imply that God is qualitatively more present in the sacred than in the secular? As we will see later, a careful reflection on the African Christian worldview reveals them to be people of a deep spiritual or religious orientation.

It is suggested that the term, spirituality has both a personal or specific use as well as a general use. Its specific use describes a longing for something beyond the merely material. It has to do with finding meaning and value in life and attempts to answer questions about one's very existence. It is therefore not merely about religious discourse but an embodiment of reflections on what makes life worth living. On the other hand, its general use includes the life of the whole person. It personifies the totality of the individual in relation to him/herself, to God, to nature or environment, and to others in relation to God. As an embodiment of the human personality in relation, it enables one to look beyond oneself and attempts to answer the question, *How can a person know God in such a way as to make sense of life?* It is suggested that spirituality refers to the actualization of human self-transcendence, that is, one's capacity for relating, for knowing, and for committing oneself to whatever is acknowledged as the ultimate, the holy, or a higher power, or God.[237] It therefore encompasses the physical, emotional, spiritual and whatever makes life worth living.

As one considers an argument for the centrality of spirituality, Albers affirms the need for a simultaneous

---

[237] See Joann Wolski Conn. "Spirituality and Personal Maturity," in *Clinical Handbook of Pastoral Counselling*, Volume 1, Expanded Edition, ed. Robert J. Wicks, Richard D. Parsons and Donald Capps. Mahwah, NJ: The Paulist Press, 1993, pp. 37-57.

affirmation of "wholism" in defining spirituality. For Albers, "spirituality involves the inexplicable relational dimension of the Divine-human encounter experienced at the center of one's being." This is, however, not narrowed "to the one-to-one-relationship alone, but can and often does involve a communal dimension."[238] Bradley Holt, in *Thirsty for God*, notes:

> How one understands spirit will determine how one understands spirituality. For example, if spirit is separated from physical reality, in a realm of its own, apart from the daily life of human experience, the resulting spirituality will become an escape into another world . . . Humans are not divided but, rather, are unities of body, mind, and spirit. The result is that spirituality has a much more wholistic and down-to-earth meaning. It encompasses the whole of human life and will develop in a variety of styles, depending on cultures, denominations, personalities, and gifts.[239]

For Holt, spirituality need not be divorced from the real and concrete realities of life's ecstasies and exigencies. To this end, an argument needs to be made for the care not only of the total person, but the care of the total system of which that person is a part.[240] According to Anne Carr:

> Spirituality can be described as the whole of our deepest religious beliefs, convictions, and patterns of thought, emotion, and behaviour in respect to what is ultimate, to God. Spirituality is holistic, encompassing our relationships to all of creation—to others, to society and nature, to work and recreation—in a fundamentally religious orientation.[241]

Spirituality is therefore comprehensive and all-encompassing, reaching into one's unconscious depths, and thus more than a conscious moral code. It shapes behaviour and attitude, and in

---

[238] Albers, "Spirituality and Religion," p. 1f.
[239] Bradley Holt. *Thirsty for God*, Minneapolis: Augsburg Press, 1993, p. 5.
[240] Albers, *Continuity and Change*, p. 4.
[241] Anne Carr. "On Feminist Theology," in *Spirituality. Ministry and Field Education*. Key Resources: Volume V. Ed. Donald Beisswenger, Doran McCarty and Lynn Rhodes. Nashville and San Francisco: The Association for Theological field Education, 1986, p. 31.

relation to God, reflects who we really are, our deepest selves. Hence it is pivoted on a person's life and activity in relation to God, to oneself, and to others in reference to God. How then can a person refer to God?

From an African Christian perspective, unlike missionary spirituality which seeks to separate the sacred from the secular,[242] it is erroneous to suggest that God is more qualitatively present in the sacred than in the secular. We can deduce from the above that spirituality pervades the totality of human existence and endeavour. Consequently, Bishop Sarpong is quoted to have said, "To the African, religion is like the skin that you carry along with you wherever you are, not like the cloth that you wear now and discard . . . the next moment."[243] This suggests that God's presence and activity permeates both the sacred and the secular, and wherever one chooses to encounter God.

Generally speaking, the expression of spirituality is through the body community according to its occurrence and experience in history. Skhakhane in his essay, *African Spirituality* thereby suggests that spirituality is concerned with life as a whole. For him, spirituality is not a pious behaviour but rather a commitment and involvement in a manner that gives meaning to life; that which influences a person to live in a way and manner which is really fulfilling. This kind of fulfillment is lived within a community, which is certainly the core of spirituality. Community, here, includes not only the living but also the ancestors and "includes the state of the whole family."[244] Such a keen sense of community from which fulfillment is derived is where roles are assigned and the quest for humanity is very much emphasized in relationships.

Africans generally express and live their spirituality through their culture. Their health systems are structured through their cosmology.[245] According to Masamba ma Mpolo, "culture is the place where Homo-Africanus and the divine encounter each other in a network of relationships, representations, symbolisms

---

[242] Masamba ma Mpolo, *Spirituality and Counselling*, p. 17.

[243] Masamba ma Mpolo, *Spirituality and Counselling*, p. 16.

[244] J. Skhakhane. "African Spirituality," in *The Church and African Culture*, ed. M. Makobane *et al.* Germiston: Lumko, 1995, p. 106-112.

[245] K.A. Busia. "The African Worldview," in *Christianity and African Culture: The Proceedings of a Conference held in Accra, Gold Coast, May 2-6, 1955* (Christian Council of Gold Coast, 1955) p. 1.

and rituals."[246] Thus, authentic Christian spirituality in concrete expression of healing and wholeness must consider one's culture. For K. A. Busia, "the uniqueness of man lies in the fact that he alone has culture." He goes on to succinctly elucidate culture to include political, economic, kinship, educational and religious institutions — all the modes of thought and behaviour, all the experience, the entire social heritage which are handed down from one generation to another through communication, interaction, and learning.[247] Kofi Asare Opoku suggests that culture is a God-given heritage which can be understood as the sum total of all traditions, ideas, customs, modes of behaviour, patterns of thought, ways of doing things and outlook on life that have been received from God, learned and passed on from one generation of Africans to the other.[248] Thus, "a spirituality which does not incorporate all people, their events, their richness, their hopes and concerns cannot speak to Africans who are fundamentally communal and relational."[249] African Christian spirituality is therefore expressed through rituals and symbols and interpreted by its own anthropological and religious suppositions. This thought is explored further in the next section as we consider the worldview of the Ewe people of southeastern Ghana.

It is, however, worth noting that spirituality, though not against religion, looks beyond religion to encompass the culture and traditions of the people. It is consequently sometimes identified with narrative experiences or cultural categories such as myths, legends and folklores. One's relationship with a higher transcendent power or God influences and determines one's relationship with others and helps one to know him/herself better. Accordingly, the commitment to this superior power becomes primary in determining one's spirituality. Spirituality is about values and helps shape one's values. It is influenced by religion and one's belief about human nature. For this reason, it is absolutely essential that this concept of wholism be emphasized in considering wholeness for the alcoholic and for those affected.

---

[246] Masamba ma Mpolo, *Spirituality and Counselling*, p. 18.

[247] Busia, *The African Worldview*, p. 1.

[248] Kofi Asare Opoku. *West African Traditional Religion.*

[249] A. Bellagamba. "New Attitudes Towards Spirituality," in *Towards African Christian Maturity*, ed. Alyward Shorter. Kampala: St. Paul, 1987, p. 107.

Significance of Religion

Just as the meaning of spirituality is often fuzzy, religion is also difficult to define. This is because its meaning is often characterized by individual perceptions or experiences. Such experiences often move beyond the individual to encompass communal experiences. Generally, however, despite their seeming diametrically opposed intentions, religion, just like spirituality, has to do with the individual's relationship with Ultimate Deity as expressed in rituals and symbols.

> The word "religion" conjures up a multiplicity of ideas and images. For some people it is intellectual assent to some given set of propositional truths which are held sacred. For others it connotes a prescribed set of rites and rituals which may be associated with critical, transitional or significant milestones throughout the life cycle. Still others associate religion with a particular deity that comes to expression both in attitude and in action in relationship to God, others, nature and oneself. Many people will assert that religion is a combination of a belief system, coupled with ritual which comes to expression in a particular lifestyle. This lifestyle is commensurate with the norms and values that the individual or group holds as sacred.[250]

Ghunney also quotes Walter Clark, one of the greatest psychologists of religion, as suggesting that "religion can be characteristically described as the inner experience of the individual when he senses a beyond."[251] Also, Sigmund Freud is quoted to have stated that, "religion developed from the need to exorcise the terrors of nature, particularly the cruelty of death, and also to make amends for the deprivations that culture imposes on the individual."[252] These definitions seek to affirm religion as the individual's perception of the infinite as having control over their destiny and thereby entitled to obedience, reverence and worship. Whatever one considers as the ultimate, divine, or infinite is so transcendent that one needs to anchor one's faith and personality to it and constantly adjust one's inner

---

[250] Albers, *Spirituality and Religion*, p.2.
[251] Ghunney, *African Spirituality*.
[252] Ghunney, *African Spirituality*.

experiences thereto. Due to its transcendence, it is believed to constructively transform the moral character, and values of its adherents, and also inform their relationships with the world. It is therefore lived in daily life experiences; hence a functional part of one's culture. Accordingly, Talcott Parsons is noted to have suggested:

> Religion is the point of articulation between cultural systems and social systems. It is also a vehicle through which cultural values are embodied in the society and are externalized in the personality system.[253]

Thus, religion can be said to reflect norms and traditions that groups adhere to and can therefore not be reflected on without cognizance of the history and culture of the people. In this case therefore, the relationship between sacred myths and objective reality is very close and one cannot be considered without the other. For this reason, Ghunney postulates that "religion is a human phenomenon that functions to unite cultural, social and personality systems into a meaningful whole, the experience of which is through ritual and worship."[254]

The African idea about God is praxis oriented. God is not considered as an abstract supernatural being but one who has been experienced. For the African, spirituality and religion is about everyday experience and not just a cognitive perception. Since African Traditional Religion attempts to deal with everyday life, one's spirituality can therefore not be considered outside the context of one's religious worldview. According to Gyekye, "to be born into the African society is to be born into a culture that is intensely and pervasively religious."[255]

The African worldview consequently suggests that spirituality encompasses both the seen and the unseen, the spiritual and the material, the mundane and the holy. There is therefore no distinction between the sacred and the secular. Lartey suggests that in Ghana, to find meaning and solutions to problems of whatever sort, due cognizance must be taken of

---

[253] Ghunney, *African Spirituality.*
[254] Ghunney, *African Spirituality.*
[255] Kwame Gyekye. *African Cultural Values: An Introduction.* Accra, Ghana: Sankofa Publishing Company, 2003, p. 4.

one's spirituality or religious worldview. [256] To this end, Baeta writes:

> Traditionally in Ghana, the solution to all problems of ill-health, as of concern or anxiety generally has been sought squarely within the framework of religion. On a worldview which assumes the effective presence of numberless spirits, and regards all life as one; with no clear distinctions between material and non material, the natural and the supernatural let alone the secular and the religious; or even between man and other created beings, this could hardly be otherwise.[257]

The presence of the ultimate or divine is therefore acknowledged in every sphere of the communal or individual life of the African. Religion is said to be at the root of African culture and thus, "religion is life and life, religion."[258] To therefore reflect on the culture or worldview of African people is to reflect on their relationship with God. This harmonious relationship within and between human beings and the spirit world, is explored further as we consider the communal nature of the African family in the next chapter. It is, however, very relevant to consider at this stage the place of the church in the quest for wholeness.

The African Christian Church, Healing, and Wholeness

The place of the church in the process of restoration and wholeness is very foundational and cannot be overlooked. The Hebrew word *shalom,* which connotes harmony and also wholeness or well-being in all dimensions, also includes good health. In the same way, the Greek, *soteria,* which translates as salvation also means to heal or to be delivered from danger and illness. It is generally God's work of deliverance for humankind

---

[256] Emmanuel Lartey. "Some Contextual Implications for Pastoral Counselling in Ghana," in *Pastoral Care and Counselling in Africa Today,* Jean Masamba ma Mpolo and Daisy Nwachuku, Eds., Frankfurt am Main: Peter Lang, 1991, p. 38.

[257] C.G. Baeta. *Christianity and Healing.* Ibadan: ORITA, 1967, p. 51. See also A.A. Berinyuu, *Pastoral Care to the Sick in Africa,* Frankfurt: Peter Lang, 1988.

[258] Kofi Asare Opoku. *West African Traditional Religion.* Nigeria: FEP International Private Limited, 1978, p. 1.

and thereby regarded as a primary function of the church.[259] This affirms the fact that the church has as its basic function, healing and wholeness for all persons, including alcoholics. This is, however, not without its challenges.

Missionary Christianity is said to have placed the African at a crossroad in reference to one's beliefs and practices. According to Williamson, the principal responsibility of the missionaries was "the destruction of traditional superstition and the implantation of the Christian faith."[260] They attempted to draw people away from their traditional life and patterns of living so as to accept European culture. The church sought to encourage converts to denounce the old for the new: to denounce "traditional religion with its corporate outlook and corporate responsibility for the Christian faith with its stress on individual responsibility." For the missionaries, traditional beliefs and practices were evil, hence people were urged to denounce evil of every form.[261] Such thought patterns influenced their processes to the extent that government influence and authority was also used to superimpose the Christian faith on the indigenes, and to break down family or communal systems and also traditional cultural practices.

The Christian religion in this case did not seem to meet the real and vital spiritual need of the African, the total well-being in all dimensions. This really affected the church's stability or impact among the indigenes. Williamson notes that the issue of importance is not whether the church has been established, but what kind of church and whether it is integrated with Akan society and able to meet in a real and vital fashion, spiritual need.[262] According to Mercy Oduyoye:

> The missionary told the Africans what they needed to be saved from, but when Africans need power to deal with the spiritual realms that were real to them, the missionary

[259] Abraham Akrong. *African Religions, Media and Health: An Overview.* Unpublished Paper Presented at the World Association for Christian Communication Conference on Religion, Media and Health in West Africa at GIMPA, Accra: December 4, 2006, p. 1.
[260] Sidney George Williamson. *Akan Religion and the Christian Faith: A Comparative Study of the Impact of Two Religions,* ed. Kwesi Dickson. Accra, Ghana: Ghana Universities Press, 1965, p. 1.
[261] Williamson, *Akan Religion,* p. 149.
[262] Williamson, *Akan Religion,* p. 73.

was baffled. The ancestors were to be ignored; infant mortality and premature deaths were purely medical matters, failure of rains and harvests were acts of God. Childlessness had nothing to do with witchcraft, nor was there any spiritual aspect to any other physical disorder or infirmity . . . The missionaries' superficial assessment of the indigenous culture and its hold on the people who belong to it led to the African's superficial acceptance of Christianity.[263]

This attempt to change the African from their worldview resulted in some converted Christians accepting Christianity superficially and thus not able to enter the soul world of the African.[264] According to Williamson, this places the African Christian in "two un-reconciled levels." The members of the church were there for the sake of its benefits and discipline rather than loyalty and fellowship. Thus, "below the system of conscious beliefs are deeply embedded traditions and customs implying quite a different interpretation of the universe and the world of spirits from Christian interpretation."[265] This situation is indeed baffling for the African Christian as well.

Africans are indeed a practical people and their spirituality is undeniably practical and experienced in relation to the cosmos and within the context of community. The Christian faith as planted by the early western missionaries among Africans has "proved unable to sympathize with or relate its message spiritually to the Akan spiritual outlook, thus dulling its impact."[266] This situation clearly puts the African Christian at a defining moment in the hands of religion.

The church has on her hands communities of believers whom, by and large, live ambivalent spiritual lives. Christianity to them is a fashionable religion which has the habit of beginning and ending within the walls of a church building.[267]

[263] Mercy Amba Oduyoye, *Hearing and Knowing: Theological Reflections on Christianity in Africa.* Maryknoll, New York: Orbis Books, 1986, p. 41.

[264] See also J.S. Pobee. *Toward an African Theology.* Nashville: Abingdon Press, 1979.

[265] Williamson, *Akan Religion,* p. 160.

[266] Williamson, *Akan Religion,* p. 175.

[267] E.B. Idowu. "The Predicament of the Church in Africa," in *Christianity in*

In order to meet the real and vital spiritual needs of the African Christian in an environment where evil is considered hyperactive, Asamoah-Gyadu notes that "African Christians have found pentecostal/charismatic theologies of dominion and alleviation of suffering relevant in their struggles with fears and insecurities."[268]

In *Translating the Devil: Religion and Modernity Among the Ewe in Ghana*, Birgit Meyer notes how the inability of older mission churches to take the experience of the Holy Spirit seriously to "ward off or cast out evil spirits" and offer people "protection and healing" in His power are the causes of drifts into Pentecostalism.[269] Asamoah-Gyadu further explains this phenomenon when he notes that Pentecostal spirituality as a form of religious expression, especially in its contemporary charismatic forms, is popular in Africa partly because its interpretations and responses to evil are not discontinuous with traditional religious aspirations.[270]

In connection with life, evil is generally considered as that which prevents people from living life in its totality. This is emphasized in both traditional and indigenous Christian worldviews. For Meyer, the performance of traditional ritual, as "the pivot of religious life" is aimed at achieving "health, fertility, protection and success in life."[271] To this end, in the process of conversion, the Ewe Christians "measured the success of Christianity by its capacity to counteract evil at least as successfully as Ewe religion."[272]

Pentecostalism, according to Asamoah-Gyadu, "provides the ritual context within which the consequences of evil may be dealt with." This is customarily emphasized in healing and deliverance phenomena which is not restricted to that tradition. "Underlying all the religious pilgrimages in search of divine intervention from evil is a certain belief that in this world, things

Africa, ed. C.G. Baeta. Oxford: Oxford University Press, 1968, p. 433.

[268] J. Kwabena Asamoah-Gyadu. "Conquering Satan, Demons, Principalities, and Powers" in *African Religions: A Ghanaian Perspective on Religion, Evil and Deliverance*, n.d., p. 1.

[269] Birgit Meyer. *Translating the Devil: Religion and Modernity Among the Ewe in Ghana*. Trenton, NJ: Africa World Press, 1999, p. 133,134.

[270] Asamoah-Gyadu, *Conquering Satan*, p.1f.

[271] Meyer, *Translating the Devil*, pp. 61, 68.

[272] Meyer, *Translating the Devil*, p. 138.

do not happen by chance, and that people need supernatural intervention in order to cope with the phenomenon of evil." This statement proceeds on the premise that traditional notions of mystical causality and the creation of ritual contexts for wrestling with evil define religious activity in Ghana, and to a large extent African life as a whole.[273] Thus, the search for meaning within the context of religion is fundamental because, for the African, there is no distinction between the secular and the sacred. This quest for survival in the African traditional context is therefore not a mindset which is alien to the religious world of the Bible.[274]

Within the Ghanaian Christian context, therefore, religion serves as a survival strategy. For the Christian church to consider health and wholeness for its people the holistic conception of illness must be considered and the church must essentially consider the view of mystical causality which is significantly established in the worldview of the people.

Spiritual healing in the Christian context is a process in which healing is achieved through the working of the Holy Trinity, appropriated through faith and admonished through prayers and liturgical processes that include the use of certain religious symbols or elements such as water and anointing oil. In the African Independent Churches, very much like traditional culture, the "*raison d'être* of religion is to gain access to spiritual power that can help human beings to overcome the forces that can disrupt life."[275]

Against this backdrop of mystical causality, healing in Africa often tends to be a function of religion. Consequently, "in an attempt to bridge the gap between western cerebral theology and the African experience, indigenous churches of Pentecostal/charismatic persuasions in particular make healing and exorcism the center of their ministries."[276] According to Emmanuel Lartey, people visit traditional hospitals when they

---

[273] Asamoah-Gyadu, *Conquering Satan*, p. 8.
[274] See Ephesians 6:11-12. "Put on the full armor of God so that you can stand against the devil's schemes. Our struggle is not against flesh and blood, but against the rulers, against the authorities, against the powers of the dark world and against spiritual forces of evil in the heavenly realms."
[275] Akrong, *African Religions, Media and Health*, p. 5.
[276] Emmanuel Lartey. "Healing: Tradition and Pentecostalism in Africa Today." *International Review of Mission*, vol. 75, no 297, 1986, p. 75.

are sick, but particularly when the problems persist, they are likely to visit one of the many healing camps or prayer meetings held around the country in search of God's intervention. This situation renders African Pentecostal/charismatic churches culturally and religiously amenable to the masses of people who find in them congenialities absent from the non-interventionist theologies of the historic mission denominations.[277] Asamoah-Gyadu in *Rethinking African Worldviews of Mystical Causality*, however, observes that though it was initially rejected by historic western mission denominations because they dismissed African fears of witchcraft and demonic affliction as figments of people's imagination or psychological delusions and did not consider it an integral part of mission, "attitudes have changed with the realization that there are phenomenological similarities between healing and deliverance ministries and African traditional priest-healers."[278] Both groups, however, operate within the context of the general African Traditional worldview of mystical causation and healing is aimed at restoring one into the state which he/she has been created to be. This state of freedom is consummated in the Christian concepts of faith, hope and love, which are significant elements, needed for total recovery for the alcoholic and their family.

---

[277] Lartey, *Healing*, p. 75.
[278] Asamoah-Gyadu. *Rethinking African Worldviews of Mystical Causality*, p. 5-6.

3

The Worldview of the Ewes of Southeastern Ghana

It is very important for this study to be context specific so as to provide a setting for the study. According to Emmanuel Lartey,

> Context has a highly significant influence upon behaviour and belief. As such, behaviours and beliefs need to be understood and analyzed within their context. To express sameness in response to issues from different contexts is to lose sight of the strength of this influence.[279]

For this reason, it is obligatory to explore the worldview or ethos of the people as practised by and through the communities of faith. "Caring acts are culture bound and the rationale for such acts is equally influenced by cultural and social considerations."[280] Africa is a very large continent and though its people have somewhat identical cultures, it will be erroneous to assume that all Africans have the same tradition and culture. Even within a country like Ghana, the norms and mores within a particular tribe are radically different from another although there are still a lot of commonalities which might call for generalization. In recognizing such diversities, Horton notes:

> All responsible scholars working in sub-Saharan Africa acknowledge the enormous and fascinating diversity of worldviews and thought patterns nourished by the myriad communities of the continent. One would indeed be lacking in normal human sensitivity if one were not more than a little daunted by this diversity . . . Despite the limitations posed by the wide range of cultural diversity in Africa, there are common threads which make generalization possible.[281]

---

[279] Emmanuel Lartey. *Pastoral Theology in an Intercultural World*, p.11.
[280] Lartey, *Pastoral Theology*, p. 3.
[281] R. Horton. "Tradition and Modernity Revisited." In Hollis, M. and Lukes, S. Eds. *Rationality and Relativism*, Oxford: Basil Blackwell Ltd, 1982 p. 205.

This chapter therefore involves a search for an understanding of the worldview or beliefs and practices of the Ewes of southeastern Ghana as they seek harmony in life through care for themselves and in their quest to maintain a dynamic balance in their families and communities.

The Worldview of the Ewes of Southeastern Ghana

The traditional worldview of the Ewes of southeastern Ghana is characterized by a set of beliefs and practices which are a consequence of such beliefs. To understand Ewe culture is to reflect on the Ewe religious worldview. Fayose emphasizes this when he suggests that the Ewes are highly religious and their cultural heritage is greatly influenced by their religion.[282] We can herein surmise that one's worldview which reflects one's cultural conceptions invariably informs, influences, stimulates, and propels individuals toward attaining wholeness and for that matter, maintaining a dynamic balance in life.

Among the Ewes of southeastern Ghana, their worldview which is a quintessence of a religious person seeks to reflect a meaning and a goal. The desire to unite permanently with the sacred "makes unacceptable to this worldview any value-system which thrives on profanity, the rejection of other-worldly reality defining this worldly life."[283] This worldview sees the sacred as comprising a number of spirit entities both human (ancestors) and non-human (deities, spirit beings) all presided over by an ultimate manifestation of the sacred God.[284] Though this may suggest *Polytheism*, denoting that the people also owe simultaneous allegiance to more than one object of worship, including a spontaneous allegiance to God, the originator of the universe, *it does not suggest equal status to all sacred beings including the Creator.* Perhaps other beings who are worshipped may be seen as God's vicegerents or agents through which humans communicate with the Supreme Being. Thus, worship ultimately belongs to God, *Mawuga, Se,* or *Segbolisa* alone, who

---

[282] Cyril Fayose. *Healing Our Wounds: A Ghanaian Christian Perspective on Intractable Conflict.* A PhD dissertation (St. Paul, Minnesota, 2001) p. 88.

[283] Gaba, *Religious Life,* p. 99.

[284] Gaba, *Religious Life,* p. 100.

is spirit, omniscient, omnipresent, and omnipotent.

Hence, all values in this milieu must be of sacred origin directly or indirectly.[285] Gaba in an interview suggests that in this worldview religion is indispensable. "It is a sacred worldview and human existence is based on theocracy."[286] This supposition affirms our earlier avowal that God is qualitatively present in both the sacred and the secular since the sacred or real ultimately eclipse the unreal. The fundamental human value of the sacred is objectified in issues governing all aspects of life — secular, profane, political, social, economic, medical, educational, recreational and even the formally religious dimensions. The sacred is essential and tantamounts to whatever promotes life and unity. On the other hand, whatever seeks to disrupt life, be it from human actions or activities of the deities, is considered evil. This idea seeks to emphasize the fact that God is not an intangible mystic or paranormal being but one who must be experienced. Meaning and value in life, and for that matter, wholeness, can only be attained through a meaningful relation with the real or sacred. It is this idea which is also reflected in Ewe thought about the divinities.

Thus, Ewe culture, as suggested, includes the belief in the existence of a Supreme Being, minor deities, ancestors and a host of spirit entities; the importance of kinship, marriage and family, regard for ethics and moral values, and festivals, among others. This accentuates the fact that their social life cannot be estranged from their religious ideations and practices.

The Supreme Being

Among the Ewes of Ghana, as in all African religions, there is the belief in a Supreme Being, God, who is the origin of all things, Creator and Proprietor of the universe and to whom all creatures owe allegiance and their dependence. God as supreme signifies God's sovereignty as an ultimate, uncreated, and self-existent being in whom all things end up and upon whom all things are dependent. Thus, as supreme, God is transcendent and yet is immanent and dependable. God is seen as good, just, and God's

---

[285] Gaba, *Religious Life*, p. 99.
[286] Interview with Prof. Christian Gaba at Cape Coast on 16 March, 2007.

providence for His people is believed to be complete, indiscriminate and unfailing. These ideas about the sovereignty of God are reflected in the principal names and titles ascribed to God: *Mawu*, God, *Mawuga* — the Great God, and *Se* — (The Law), the Supreme One.

The experiential nature of Ewe religious worldview is unprecedented.[287] The experience of the ultimate divine providence and goodness of God (*Mawu, Se*), is not only limited to rituals and symbols, but is often incorporated or reflected in the local names given to children to express this goodness, omnipotence and transcendence as concretely experienced in daily life situations. Among the Ewes of Ghana are such names as *Mawunyo/Worlanyo* — God/the Creator is good or God is kind; *Mawuenyega*, God is the greatest; *Selŝame*, the Creator loves mankind, or God loves people; *Senyo*, God is kind; *Senagbe*, God is the giver of life; *Selenu*, God never sleeps; *Sefakor*, God is a comforter; and *Setutsi*, God who blesses us. These names reflect the awe in which God is held by the Ewes of Ghana, and goes further to emphasize God's presence in their lives as a *Living Reality*, to whom worship is due.[288]

The spirit of the high God is said to have two components, a female and a male. The female component is objectified by earth, *Mianor Zordzi* or *Anyigba* and is responsible for harmony, peace, care, nurture, fertility, motherhood, gentleness, creativity, forgiveness, love, rest, joy and freshness. The male spirit of God, *Mawu Lisa*, on the other hand symbolizes power, strength, labour and toughness, and controls as well as dispenses justice, steadfastness, pain and suffering, security, protection and all human strivings.[289] This concept of duality is, however, not unique to the Ewes of Ghana but to most African cultures. It has also been suggested that to avoid numerous demands from the people and to show his transcendence, Mawu retired to the skies and delegated the lesser gods to manage the world.[290]

---

[287] Kofi Asare Opoku. *West African Traditional Religion*. Lagos, Nigeria: FEP International Private Limited, 1978, p. 29.

[288] Opoku, WATR, p. 29.

[289] Kodzo Gavua. "Religious Practices" in *A Handbook of Eweland, Volume II*, Accra, Ghana: Woeli Publishing Services, 2000, p. 85.

[290] See Geoffrey Parrinder. *West African Traditional Religion*. London: The Epworth Press, 1961, p. 18.

The Lesser Gods or Deities

The deities, *trɔwo* (divinities, lesser gods, spirit beings, tutelary spirits), who share in the sacred order of the divine are, however, creatures of the Supreme God; created to "fulfill specific functions and thus did not come into existence on their own volition."[291] These spirit entities and lesser gods are also characterized by dual, positive and negative images. As creatures with specific functions, they may be male or female, good or evil, and none of them enjoys the unlimited powers ascribed to *Mawu*.[292] They are not supreme in nature but are spiritual beings that act as creatures, children, representatives, agents, superintendents and refractions of the Supreme Being and are held in high esteem.[293] These gods and spirits through which people contact and interact with the Supreme Being or the Most High God can be grouped into three broad categories. Those of celestial nature *(dzimawuwo)*; spirits of the earth *(anyigbadzinuwo*, such as the *trɔwo: the* community gods and personal gods), and spirits of the ancestors *(torŋ ɔliwo)*. The Ewes also believe in other spiritual forces that can be harnessed for good or for evil. These include witchcraft, magic, sorcery, divination and oracles.

Besides *Mawuga*, the Supreme Being, *Mawu Sogble, Mawu Sodza* and *Mawu Sowlui* also dwell in the heavens and serve as messengers of Mawuga. *Sogble* is the son of Mawuga and is said to be the violent one while *Sodza*, his wife, is the benevolent one. *Sowlui* is the god of wealth and is concerned with the distribution of money and wealth. Besides these celestial gods are also those other gods of terrestrial nature, the *trɔwo*.

The *trɔwo* serve as intermediaries or messengers of the Supreme Being, *Mawu*. Due to their nature and function, they are placed above human beings and have powers limited to their areas of competence or jurisdiction and are granted full powers to act in those areas. Together with the spirit entities, there are those which are of a communal or a personal nature,

---

[291] Opoku, WATR, p.54.

[292] Opoku, WATR, p 54.

[293] Peter K. Sarpong. *Peoples Differ: An Approach to Inculturation in Evangelization.* Legon, Ghana: Sub-Saharan Publishers, 2002, p. 96.

beneficial or harmful, and function as overseers in those areas. Some of such deities are wholly or specifically evil. Though they are feared, they are also worshipped "so that their malevolence may be warded off."[294] The *trɔ wo* are ambivalent in nature, so are the other spirit entities which also have the positive aspects which promote life. Negation of, or failure on the part of humankind to observe ritual purity, rules and taboos set by the deities, will trigger the anger of the *trɔ* upon such individuals and even communities, resulting in sickness or misfortune. Most of these lesser gods are versatile in their work and achievements but some tend to specialize. For instance, the *Nyigbla* god of the Anlo-Ewe is regarded as a war god though its activities are never limited to this.[295] As spirits, they are capable of making any nature object, such as trees, rivers, lagoons, forests, rocks, animals and the sea, their abode and have cults and shrines where the priests and priestesses conduct organized worship of the gods by their adherents. For the Ewe, therefore, power is ambivalent. As long as these forces have power to promote life, they also possess the capacity to do the contrary — disrupt life.

The Ancestors *(Tɔgbeɲɔliwo/Mamaɲɔliwo)*

The ancestral spirits occupy an important place in the socio-religio-cultural life of the Ewes of southeastern Ghana as in most African societies. They are benevolent in nature and play the role of guardians of the living. As guardians, they are also capable of punishing wrongdoings and immoral acts. They are viewed as "a great cloud of witnesses" surrounding us so as to watch over or guard the living in their life and dealings. According to Idowu:

> The ancestors are regarded still as heads and parts of the families and community to which they belonged while they were living human beings. The ancestors remain therefore, spiritual superintendents of family affairs and continue to bear their titles of relationship like "father" or "mother."[296]

---

[294] Opoku, WATR, p. 70.
[295] Nukunya, *Tradition and Change*, p. 57.
[296] E.B. Idowu. *African Traditional Religion*. London: SCM Press, 1973, p. 184.

The significance of the place of the ancestor is further buttressed by the fact that in this milieu, it has been noted that a chief derives his authority from the fact that he sits on the stool of the ancestors and represents his people before the ancestors.[297] Thus, it is not all men and women who have died that are viewed as ancestors, but those who have led exemplary lives and died honourably at an advanced age and had children. Their veneration is therefore emphasized in this respect. Prayers are offered to the ancestors at a personal, family, and communal level as in festivals. They are generally prayed to for blessings of good health, fertility, successful fishing and good harvest. Such rites and prayers are usually organized by descent groups[298] and serve as a means of social control.

> The fact that only people of certain caliber qualify as ancestors regulates behaviour by making individuals and groups not only to conform but also to lead such exemplary lives as to enable them qualify for the honour after their deaths. Again the belief in the ability of the dead to punish wrong doing and reward good behaviour helps in no small way to regulate social behaviour and serves as a challenge to people to do their best for their families, descent groups and community at large. Above all, the beliefs buttress traditional authority and enhance the positions of the chiefs, lineage heads and the elders.[299]

Other Spirit Forces (Entities)

Among the Ewes of southeastern Ghana, there is also the belief in a horde of other spiritual forces that can be harnessed for good or for evil. This includes witchcraft, magic, sorcery, divination, and oracle. Persons who are believed to possess inherent supernatural powers which they use knowingly or

---

[297] The stool is thus regarded as the ancestral shrine which is the repository of the ancestor's soul. Thus, ancestral veneration is symbolically performed through the stool of the ancestors.

[298] Descent grounds are basically groups of people with direct genealogical connections and covers an individual's offspring across generations.

[299] Nukunya, *Tradition and Change*, p. 59ff.

otherwise to harm others or for the benefit of themselves are called witches and wizards (*adzetɔwo*), though they are generally characterized as witches since they are mostly female. Magic (*dzoɖuame*) is the manipulation of physical objects for effecting good supernatural ends. Sorcery is the anti-social use of magic, that is, the manipulation of physical objects to cause evil supernatural ends. Its popular connotation is *juju* or black magic. Divination (*afa kaka*) is the suitable manipulation of certain physical objects to foretell the future, discover the unknown or interpret events. For instance, the *Afa* of the Ewes of southeastern Ghana is one of the best-organized divination systems among the Ewes.[300]

Closely linked to divination are oracles or oracular consultation. An oracle is a deity, shrine or object which is reputed to have the power to reveal the unknown. These supernatural forces are employed to protect self or to enhance one's situation to harm or even kill a rival, to reveal the unknown, and to search for missing objects or meaning of events. The belief in and the fear of evil spiritual forces is so strong that it affects social behaviour and also serves as a means of social control. Besides, these spiritual realities: festivals, rites of passage, kinship and social organizations are also very significant to this worldview.

Festivals

Though it might be viewed as a social event, festivals are significant moments when Ewe beliefs and practices associated with the supernatural are manifested. Festivals are therefore a microcosm of the entire cultural heritage of a people and are generally organized around lineage stools, clan gods, and town or village deities; and may also commemorate special events, both secular and religious. Though there are several important festivals among the Ewes of southeastern Ghana, the *Hogbetsotso* festival of the Anlo-Ewe is the most outstanding. The *Hogbetsotso* is deeply rooted in history, tradition and culture. It is basically a re-enactment of the migration of the Anlo-Ewes of southeastern

---

[300] Nukunya, *Tradition and Change*, p. 59ff.

Ghana from Notsie in Togo where they lived under a cruel King Agokoli. In the case of *Hogbetsotso*, as with other Ewe festivals, besides the re-enactment of the historical event and its related incidents, the main religio-cultural activities include *dɔdede* (removal of disease through general cleaning and expulsion of evil spirits), *nugbidodo* (general reconciliation), *hanud/udu* (openhouse parties), and drumming and dancing. *Dɔdede* which literally means "removal of disease" is a ritual purification rite to expel not only diseases but also the evil spirits behind those diseases. It precedes the celebration and is in preparation for communion with *Mawu* and the other deities. *Nugbidodo* is a rite for fostering harmony, peace and reconciliation, which is a precondition for the success of the festival since the ancestors do not like their kinsfolk to remain in disharmony and the gods also abhor enmity and breach in relationships which hinders progress and may lead to ill-health. Also of extreme significance and closely related to *nugbidodo* is *hanud/udu* or communal meal, which is a sign of good neighbourliness, bonding and a manifestation of harmony among the kinsfolk.[301] Through these processes, bridges are built or restored, not only between humans but also with the spirit world. Traditional values and other elements of culture are also handed down from one generation to another.

Rites of Passage

Rites of passage have to do with the periods of transition that characterize an individual's growth and development from one stage to another. It helps alleviate the crises that epitomize such transitions, and also helps prepare people for such transitions which are generally typified by rites and rituals by way of celebrations. From the cradle to the grave, from the womb to the tomb, the landmarks of the individual's life cycle are birth, puberty, marriage and death.

The celebrations or rituals that portray these stages also shed light on traditional Ewe religious ideals and beliefs. These

---

[301] G. K. Nukunya. "Festivals," in *A Handbook of Ewe Land. Volume I: The Ewes of Southeastern Ghana*, ed. Francis Agbodeka. Accra: Woeli Publishing Services, 1997, p. 105-108.

ceremonies emphasize the importance of the family and are therefore done within the context of the family and community in which the person is born. They serve as moments of impartation of values, recognition, acceptance and affirmation of the individual's positions and roles as members of a family and community. Such rites seek to help one to believe in one's self and in the ideals of one's family. Moral laws and norms of the community are also inculcated into the youth and the consequences of breach of such laws are also emphasized. As a very social people who love to socialize, these rites as in other ceremonies, are characterized by singing, drumming and dancing. They are communal in nature and help to renew one's ties to the family and community. In this process, the achievements of the ancestors are sometimes replayed and one's relation with the Supreme Being and other deities is developed. One therefore becomes conscious of one's self in relation to God, to the deities, and to others in the community, while being reminded of one's roles and responsibility to the family and duty to God and others.

One significant characteristic feature of these rites of passage, as in festivals, is the emphasis on libation. This presupposes that ancestors are not left out of such celebrations and failure to honour them on such occasions could invoke their wrath.

> Libations are poured to achieve both communion and propitiation. The family ancestors are called upon at the important moments of life: birth, puberty, marriage, and death; they are also called upon on occasions when new ventures are being undertaken, e.g. travel, trade or building. In situations of grave importance to the clan or ethnic group the ancestors cannot be left out. Those who have gone before have a part to play in preserving family ties and are often called upon to be witnesses at the reconciliation of estranged members of a community. This is the language of the people which conveys their understanding of the universe, of participation with the living and the dead and life beyond the physical death.[302]

---

[302] Lartey, *Some Contextual Implications*, p. 40.

This recognition of the ancestors as ever present in and influencing their daily lives must not be erroneously construed as worship of ancestors. They are not considered as gods and are not worshipped as gods.[303] As protectors of life and the community, they must be recognized as part of the systemic network of relationships and therefore venerated.

Kinship and Family Organization

Kinship is the means through which socio-political organization of the Ewes of southeastern Ghana could be understood. According to Nukunya, "kinship refers to social relationships derived from consanguinity, marriage and adoption."[304] The importance of kinship is in the fact that it determines almost everything. It determines political, religious, economic, legal, ethical, and social relations. Membership is based on patrilineal descent in clans and lineages.

> The kinship system *prescribes statuses* and roles to people who are in particular relationships. It determines the rules, duties and obligations of individuals and groups in all aspects of life in which these individuals and groups interact. Thus it is the kinship system, for instance, which determines where the couple will live after marriage, how property will be transmitted, who succeeds whom and even who should worship at a particular shrine.[305]

Kinship plays a key role in political organization. The rules and principles of seniority, succession, and residence pattern are governed by the kinship system. It is the descent group that organizes ancestral rites. The kinship system determines who will worship at a particular shrine, the person who will officiate, which ancestral spirit should be invoked, and where the rites and rituals should be performed. Ethics and etiquette as well as inheritance, property relations, residence patterns, and other economic relations are determined by the kinship system. Kinship

---

[303] Berinyuu, *Pastoral Care to the Sick in Africa*, p. 8.
[304] Nukunya, *Tradition and Change*, p. 18.
[305] Nukunya, *Tradition and Change*, p. 18.

determines the respective positions of men and women in society, of old and young, father and child, mother and child, as well as husband and wife, among others. Incest, for instance, is defined within the context of kinship.

Nukunya suggests that kinship plays a greater role in the more homogenous rural communities of the Ewes than in urban situations. Social mobility and spatial change tend to diminish its importance and people no longer depend on lineage property; status is no longer dependent on age or a person's position in the kinship system; *gender roles are not maintained*, and kinship groups are no longer localized. However, kinship still plays a significant role among urban dwellers and is acknowledged and comes alive in times of crises such as in a medical emergency, death, or a funeral and marriage as well.

There are two main descent groups, namely *clans* and *lineages*. The clan (*Hlɔ̃*) may be described as a group of people who are believed to have descended patrilineally from a common ancestor and share the same totemic and other observances.[306] Membership is normally obtained by birth but in the past strangers and slaves were sometimes incorporated into the clans of their host or masters and accorded full membership. Although they are scattered, clans are corporate in nature and have a common ancestor or ancestress. They own land, appoint leaders who are vested with legal and ritual powers, meet regularly to discuss matters of common interest; have their own shrines, and are usually held responsible for the wrongs of its members. The lineage is that segment of the clan found in one locality. Within the same locality, the relationships of clan folks are more frequent and effective.

Marriage is another means of becoming a member of a kinship group. Through the institution of marriage, kinship is both established and extended. It is therefore a basic establishment of the Ewe society. Because the kinship system strictly regulates marriage, marriage is said to be contracted between families and not individuals. The marriage process involves elaborate prescriptions, procedures and prohibitions, and also entails certain rights and obligations. Family is the end

---

[306] An ethnic group on the other hand is defined in relation to language.

result of the marriage process. As has been suggested earlier, the family is the micro-unit of the clan or descent group. Thus members of a family are involuntary members of a kinship group.

Kinship behaviours are sanctioned by the supernatural, particularly the dead (*torgbeŋoliwo*) who monitor the activities of the living. Anyone who destabilizes or causes variance or disharmony in the kin group is severely punished through illness, bad harvest and even death. The danger of invoking such calamities on one's self ensures good morals and behaviour compatible with the norms and mores of the community.[307]

In Africa no one is viewed in isolation. "Nobody is an island." As suggested, everyone is viewed in relation to the family to which one belongs. The family is one concept which is not easy to define due to the fact that in Ghana, it is also still a part of larger systems called clans and lineages as reflected under kinship. For Nukunya, "Kinship is the key to understanding of traditional societies,"[308] and could be seen as "the totality of relationships based on consanguinity, affinity, and adoption."[309] Clans and lineages are therefore descent groups under kinship. In whatever context it is viewed, they all seek to reflect one's origins and the genealogical connections between members. Thus, in talking about family of origin in the traditional Ghanaian context, one could go as far as to look at lineages.

The interconnection of clan members and lineages is very much emphasized in this context. However, depending on the region or ethno-area one comes from, these kinship systems could be matrilineal or patrilineal; unilineal or bilineal. Thus, potentially, an individual can use many ties, but only one of the ties, usually, can be utilized at any given time for descent purposes.[310] This is what, however, determines one's pattern of inheritance. Due to its genealogical connections, in the traditional Ghanaian worldview, "descent groups serve as pillars

---

[307] See Nukunya, "Social and Political Organization," in *A Handbook of Eweland: The Ewes of Southeastern Ghana*, pp. 47-84; also *Tradition and Change in Ghana: An Introduction to Sociology*, p. 20ff.

[308] G.K. Nukunya. *Tradition and Change in Ghana: An Introduction to Sociology*, second edition. Accra, Ghana: Ghana Universities Press, 2003, p. 17.

[309] Nukunya, *Tradition and Change*, p. 40.

[310] Nukunya, *Tradition and Change*, p. 39.

around which most societies are built."[311] Though we have sought to emphasize this in the general context, the relationship of affinity has not been so much emphasized. This is because though affinity is an aspect of kinship, its actual perspectives are manifested in marriage and the relationships that develop out of it — *the family.*

Nukunya posits that though it is not always very easy to define, generally speaking, a "family is a group of individuals related to one another by ties of consanguinity, marriage or adoption, the adult members of which are responsible for the upbringing of children."[312] Family could be categorized as nuclear or extended, a nuclear family being a married couple and their children, and this could also be monogamous or polygamous. The extended family is also built around close relatives either on patrilineal or matrilineal lines.

> Whether nuclear or extended, monogamous or poly-gamous, families can be divided into *families of orientation* and *families of procreation.* A family of orientation is the one in which the individual is a child, the one into which he or she is born while a family of procreation is the one in which the individual is a parent or adult and into which a new generation of children is brought up.[313]

To talk about one's family and for that matter, one's family of origin is to make reference to one's lineage or extended family. This is to say one's identity lies not in oneself, but the family (lineage) from which one derives. It is therefore now clear that family system thinking is useful in understanding the *identified patient* in the traditional Ghanaian family. This is because whatever the symptoms are, its derivation may not be from the individual but the family field to which he/she belongs. The individual's family is thus a subsystem of a larger system, the lineage. For this reason, in Ghana, and for that matter in all of Africa, anything that concerns an individual concerns the

---

[311] Nukunya, *Tradition and Change*, p. 59.
[312] Nukunya, *Tradition and Change*, p. 49.
[313] Nukunya, *Tradition and Change*, p. 49.

family. Thus, an individual's addictive behaviour may derive from some imbalances within the family system and has an enormous effect on the family by permeating through the entire system.

Relationality and Communality

Life is relational and the fact that spirituality pivots on relationships, presupposes that one's religion and spirituality cannot be exercised outside the context of one's environment, that is, kinship or family from which it derives. One cannot disengage oneself from the religion of the community. Doing so would mean isolating oneself from the group and disrupting one's sense of communal membership and security, thus losing much of the meaning of life.[314] This seeks to emphasize the fact that religion is not an individual affair, but a corporate or communal one, woven into the culture of the people. One therefore finds harmony in life through belonging to a larger harmony of life with others. According to Busia, "Virtue is not something which the individual can possess or enjoy independently of his fellows. A man can become, and can be truly a man only in and through his participation in culture."[315] Communal life for the African, however, incorporates the extended and the nuclear family, the living and the dead. Mtetwa notes that in African spirituality, what is envisaged is harmony in interpersonal relationships.

> One of the most remarkable and tangible dimensions of African spirituality relates to the unique notion of communality and collective solidarity that the African society exhibits in all spheres of life. There is a profound sense of interdependence, from the extended family to the entire community. In a very real sense, everybody is interrelated; including relations between the living and those who have departed.[316]

---

[314] Gyekye, *African Cultural Values*, p. 4.
[315] Busia, *The African Worldview*, p. 2.
[316] S. Mtetwa. "African Spirituality in the Context of Modernity," *Bulletin for Contextual Theology in Southern Africa & Africa* 3/2 (1996) p. 24.

Nukunya suggests that the traditional African (Ewe) family is generally characterized as an extended family. "It is, indeed, true that in Africa, family is coterminous with the extended family."[317] Nukunya's definition of a family as a group of individuals related to one another by ties of consanguinity, marriage or adoption, the adult members of which are responsible for the upbringing of children, presupposes the significant role of the family in enhancing the spiritual and moral fabric of the individual so as to maintain the dignity and integrity of the family.

It is suggested that, to maintain the link between every family and the Supreme Being, each family/household has its own deity (*fome trɔ*) that serves to reflect the presence of the Supreme Being, as an ever-present help in times of trouble. According to John Mbiti, "to be human is to belong to the whole community and to do so involves participation in the beliefs, ceremonies, rituals and festivals of that community."[318] This emphasizes the African dictum of "*Cognatus ego sum,*" meaning, "I belong, therefore I am."[319] Ghunney affirms this when he also suggests that "when the African loses his communality, he loses his personality."[320] However, the African sense of community, as suggested earlier, is not only limited to relationships between the living but that "among many Ghanaians the view is that harmony must prevail between God, the deities, the ancestors and human beings for peace, prosperity and the good life to be realized."[321] Kwesi Dickson also notes:

> The African sense of community requires the recognition of the presence of the ancestors as the rallying point of the

---

[317] G.K. Nukunya. *Tradition and Change: The Case of the Family*. Accra: Ghana Universities Press, 1972 p. 9.

[318] John Mbiti. *African Religions and Philosophy* (London: Heinemann, 1969), p. 2

[319] Joseph Kow Ghunney. *Peer Counselling Manual*, p. 30.

[320] Ghunney, "African Spirituality and Pastoral Care."

[321] Emmanuel Lartey. "Some Contextual Implications for Pastoral Counselling in Ghana." In *Pastoral Care and Counselling in Africa Today*, Jean Masamba ma Mpolo and Daisy Nwachuku, Eds. Frankfurt am Main: Peter Lang, 1991 p. 40.

group's solidarity and they, being the custodians of law and morality, may punish or reward in order to ensure the maintenance of the group's equilibrium.[322]

Thus, one cannot live in isolation of one's family or community. To reflect on one's culture is to reflect on one's family or kin group which ultimately defines one's identity. The communal nature of our "Africanness" is part of our being and when the African loses this communality, he/she loses his /her spirituality. In this context therefore, the family is a paramount reality apart from which humanity cannot exist. To detach oneself from the family is to detach oneself from one's roots or the very foundations of one's being. It is worth noting that this idea of family or community involves not only the ancestors but also the yet unborn. There are reciprocal relationships, duties and responsibilities that exist in this communal life of the family and in which behaviours are said to be sanctioned by the supernatural. Negligence of such responsibilities can result in devastating consequences and disrupt life, not only for the individual but also for the larger family. Role fulfillment in the social order is therefore of utmost importance more than personal self-actualization since one's individual identity is affirmed within the family, community or social order in which he/she has a role to play.

> Your role in society determines who you are and this is of greater importance than your personal qualities and individual needs. Role fulfillment becomes more important than personal self-actualization.[323]

The family and community thus become agents of religion where values and morals are affirmed and emphasized so as to maintain dignity and harmony in the family.

---

[322] Kwesi A. Dickson. *Theology in Africa*. London, Darton: Longman & Todd, Orbis Books, 1984, p. 70.

[323] Daniel Louw. "A Pastoral Paradigm for God-Images in an African Context," in *Spirituality and Culture in Pastoral Care and Counselling: Voices from Different Contexts*, ed. John Foskett and Emmanuel Lartey. Cardiff: Cardiff Academic Press, 2004, p. 33f.

Religion and Morality

It is worth affirming the earlier assertion that it is almost impossible to separate Ewe cultural practices from their religious beliefs. This supposition reflects their ethical life as well. Beliefs that are associated with the indigenous religion coupled with the fear of incurring the wrath and displeasure of the gods, ancestors, and other spirit beings have facilitated the upholding of discipline and the enhancing of moral and ethical values, and in so doing, sanity in the social order of the Ewes of southeastern Ghana.

Basically, the moral and ethical life of the Ewe is primarily a strict adherence to all that is virtuous and avoidance of vice of every form. Such vices are described as *ŋukpenu* (shameful acts), *busunu* (calamitous acts), and *afegbanu* (destructive acts). Practice of such *ŋukpenu*, *busunu*, and *afegbanu*, tend to bring shame not only to the individual and the family, but also incur the anger and wrath of the gods or deities against the individual, family or even entire communities. Due to the strict adherence of discipline in this community, children are taught rigorously to uphold virtue of every form and eschew all forms of vice in the community.

> Anything that would bring peace, joy and prosperity not only to the individual, but also to the community must be done. On the other hand, anything that would bring curse, sadness, sickness, death, calamity, disgrace or disrespect to the individual or the community is simply not done and must, thus, be avoided.[324]

In times past, unruly and insubordinate children were reportedly sold into slavery or given up to be killed so as to preserve the dignity of the family and the sanctity of the community.[325] The community or descent group, under the direction of *Mawuga*,

---

[324] Ted Nelson-Adjakpey. *Penance and Expiatory Sacrifice Among the Ghanaian-Ewe and their Relevance to the Christian Religion*. Rome: Tipografia Olimpica, 1982, p. 15.
[325] See F. Kwasi Fiawoo. *Toko Atolia [The Fifth Landing Stage]*. London: Longman, Green and Co. Ltd., 1962.

lesser gods and ancestors, generally dictate what is right and what must be done, and sanction what is wrong and must be avoided. This awareness obviously drives the moral and ethical life of the people. It is worth noting, however, that punishment for wrongdoing could be avenged even over the dead.

The Concept of Illness and Healthcare

Illness and disease is a normal feature of human life. Cultural diversity of given societies reflect differences in the explanation of illness and techniques in dealing with them. According to Kofi Bonsi, the medical system of any society cannot be considered in isolation of its social, political, religious and economic organization since it "is based on the same assumptions, values and worldview."[326] This is to suggest that healthcare practices are carried out within the context of values and beliefs of the people of any given society. It involves due consideration for the philosophical and religious ideas and beliefs of the people as very significant. Kodzo Senah writes that "health-seeking behaviour is influenced by the individual's explanatory model (EM) which in turn depends on the severity of the disorder and professional advice on the past."[327] This goes to affirm the earlier position of this chapter that the people's ideas on the cause of any ailment customarily dictate and direct the choice of therapy.

Among the Ewes of Ghana, perceived causes of illness and healthcare involve more than biological definitions. Cultural and metaphysical factors in illness causation cannot be negated. For the Ewes, illness causation and healthcare is pluralistic encompassing "not only the naturalistic and cultural or metaphysical but also spiritual conceptions and practices."[328] This is to say, causes of illness could therefore be natural or supernatural, physical or spiritual, and it is this idea that

---

[326] S. Kofi Bonsi. "Health Care" in *A Handbook of Eweland Vol. II*, edited by Kodzo Gavua. Accra: Woeli Publishing Services, 2000, p. 200.

[327] Kodzo Senah. "Traditional and Modern Health Care Practices" in *A Handbook of Eweland Volume I*. Accra: Woeli Publishing Services, 1997, p. 246.

[328] Bonsi, *Health Care*, p. 201.

generally dictates the choice of therapy. Treatment is therefore either natural or supernatural or both.

This worldview suggests that illness and death could result from an offence against the ancestors, violation of social taboos, an attack by deities and evil spirits, or the result of witchcraft. According to Senah, "Supernatural ailment may emanate from the wrath of God, the gods, ancestors, malevolents such as witches and sorcerers, and from breaching rituals and taboos related to clan totem or to one's personal spirit or soul (*Se* or *Klama*)."[329] Such ailments whose occurrence is uncommon and often chronic and creepy include leprosy, lunacy, ulcers, blindness, infertility and swelling diseases.[330] Alcoholism, as a chronic, fatal and progressive disease invariably falls into this category.

For Bonsi, illness can be perceived in several ways. First, it is regarded as punishment imposed by nature on a person who violates any law of hygiene or accepted way of conduct. In other words, the impaired body is a result of external dirt. Secondly, illness may be experienced as a result of imbalance in the relationship between a person and deity or the spirit world.[331] Though these two main ways may be considered as natural and supernatural, even what seems to be natural cannot be considered without reflecting on spiritual or supernatural implications; they intertwine and one cannot be considered in isolation of the other. This notwithstanding, due to the emphasis on family or kin groups, it is worth noting that any wrongdoing or negation of life by an individual can have consequences on another person or the health of the family or entire community. This thought, however, is not limited to the Ewes but is reflective of African cosmology. Masamba ma Mpolo suggests that "Sin opens the doors for life negating forces to disturb the health of the individual and to upset the ecological and entire social equilibrium."[332]

---

[329] Senah, *Traditional and Modern Health Care*, p. 247.

[330] Senah, *Traditional and Modern Health Care*, p. 247.

[331] Bonsi, *Health Care*, p. 204.

[332] Jean Masamba ma Mpolo. "Spirituality and Counselling for Healing and Liberation: The Context and Praxis of African Pastoral Activity and Psychotherapy," in *The Church and Healing: Echoes from Africa*, Emmanuel Lartey, Daisy Nwachuku, Kasonga Wa Kasonga, Eds. Frankfurt: Peter Lang, 1994, p. 23.

Diagnosis and treatment of illness and disease in this cultural milieu takes several forms which reflect both natural and supernatural dimensions. Herbalism is very common and is generally of two variations. Those that largely exclude "magico-religious" rituals on the one hand, and those that include the custodians of personal gods (*vodu*) and titular or community gods *(trɔwo)* on the other. Though these gods seek to offer protection to the individual and community, "incurring their wrath may result in the sudden visitation of deaths, diseases, plagues and famine."[333]

Gaba, however notes that the offices of a diviner, priest, and herbalist are often rolled into one since in this context, knowledge of the others is very relevant and "every little bit is a microcosm of the macrocosm."[334] Bonsi also suggests that ritual therapy among the Ewes "is based on the symbols and beliefs in the supernatural and the role ancestral spirits play in the life of the people."[335] Instructions for treatment are generally received from the deities through spirit possession or divination *(afa kaka)*.

These diviners (*bokɔwo*) whose god, *Afa* is dedicated mainly to disclosing events in the extra-sensory plane, are purported to have diagnostic skills that are very crucial in the entire healing process. This is not to suggest that bio-medicine or allopathic treatment is not an option in this milieu. In the event that allopathic and other forms of treatment fail them, they naturally turn to diviners and or medicinemen for consultations and treatment.

> The pragmatic situation is that people seek symptomatic relief from allopathic medicine, and shift quickly to other treatment regimes if it does not work, or if the condition requires the identification of the "true cause" and its management. Invariably, diagnosis reveals the wrath of God, the titular gods, ancestral spirits (*togbuiwo*), malevolent agents such as witches (*adze*), and sorcerers

---

[333] Senah, *Traditional and Modern Health Care*, p. 244f.
[334] Interview with Professor Christian Gaba at Cape Coast on 16 March, 2007.
[335] Bonsi, *Health Care*, p. 206.

(*dzotɔ*), and violation of family or community taboos (*kɔ,*
kɔdzidada) or one's personal spirit or destiny (*se/dzogbe*) as
the cause of illness.[336]

Typically, etiology as well as diagnosis asks two basic
questions: *Who is the cause of this illness? Is it I or is it someone*
else? This is also an attempt to finding answers to the general
question, *why?* In this context, organically manifested symptoms
are always the result of some aggressions and are therefore not
physically induced. What is thus essentially sought in every
illness, be it somatic or emotional, is the implication of such a
disease. Thus, though these questions are asked, the ultimate or
most fundamental question is "Why am I or my family suffering
this illness?" Diagnosis therefore searches for reasons and
announces the cause of the illness by providing its socio-
psychological and spiritual significance.[337] The consequence of
such an illness for the family and community are also pointed
to. Thus, Gaba posits that "you don't heal diseases but you heal
the whole person."[338] He notes that healing the totality of the
individual is not separated from the family or communal life; it
involves restoring harmony, peace, and unity for the ultimate
survival of the community and society as a going concern. To
this end, healing the totality of the person includes psychological,
spiritual, physical and social wellness within the context of one's
family and community.

---

[336] Bonsi, *Health Care*, p. 210; and Senah. "Traditional and Modern Health
   Practices"; also "Blofo Tsofa: Local Perception of Medicines in a Ghanaian
   Rural Community." In *Medicines: Meanings and Context*, ed. Etkin N. and M.
   Tan (Quezon City: HAIN, 1991); and also P.A. Twumasi, *Medical Systems in*
   Ghana. Tema: Ghana Publishing Corporation, 1975.
[337] Jean Masamba ma Mpolo. "A Brief Review of Psychiatric Research in Africa:
   Some Implications to Pastoral Counselling" in *Pastoral Care and Counselling*
   in Africa Today, p. 24f.
[338] Gaba, interview.

4

Alcoholism in the African Family

Introduction

This chapter attempts to summarize the results of the interviews as well as analyze and discuss the data. Each interview was guided by a set number of questions and lasted for a period of between thirty minutes and two hours. The questions were open-ended so that respondents could feel free to discuss what they saw as important. Thus, issues that the author had not earlier considered were raised by the respondents as they gave direction to the interview. The characteristics of the respondents were diverse: male, female, Christians, non-Christians, married and unmarried. For the key informants, the questions that guided the interview were:

1. What is alcoholism?
2. What are the causes of alcoholism?
3. What are the effects of alcoholism on the family?
4. What are the traditional modes of curing alcoholics?
5. What is the Ewe concept of health, wholeness and the cause of illnesses?
6. What is the significance of religion and spirituality in this context?

What is Alcoholism?

On the question of what was alcoholism, the following were responses from my informants, which seem to reflect the true nature of alcoholism as viewed by the Ewes of Southeastern Ghana:

First Informant: To say someone is an alcoholic is to mean that the person habitually drinks and forgets herself/himself and therefore is a nuisance or disgrace to the family and community.

Second Informant: Those who take hard liquor which makes them get intoxicated, making them lose their balance and cannot do what is required of them. In short, alcohol takes the better part of the person, puts him out of balance, so he cannot think or act properly. It therefore makes the person less normal and makes others feel sorry about the alcoholic's behaviour. Drink becomes a basic need for such a person, without which the person cannot live.

Third Informant: There are different types of alcoholism though some just use the word anyhow to chastise others. For some people drinking is normal but for true alcoholics they drink to feel normal, even though their drinking is abnormal and it makes them feel "normal." One can even see it from their appearance. Such people no longer have control over alcohol but alcohol controls them. The Ewes would say, *"Ame ma me gale ame me o,"* which translated literally means "Such a person is no longer a human being."

Fourth Informant: An alcoholic is someone who drinks excessively and loses control, loses his senses or forgets himself. When this continues or becomes somewhat habitual, such a person can be called an alcoholic. However one who just drinks occasionally or got drunk in one instance only but not again can't be described as an alcoholic.

Fifth Informant: Drink is a very good thing. You need it in everything that you do in life but if you abuse it, it makes you useless in society. It can make you do things you normally won't do — even kill. Thus a person who continuously drinks is not normal and so is an alcoholic. He is no longer a human being. Alcohol is good but it can destroy you if you don't respect it.

Sixth Informant: It means using alcohol in a way that makes you unproductive. To such a person alcohol is now the key to your wholeness. You can't do without it. In short, an alcoholic is one who has become a slave to alcohol.

All the informants asserted that an alcoholic is one whose drinking pattern has become a source of embarrassment to the family and community. While the second and sixth informants suggest that drink has become the basic need of the person or what makes him/her "normal," the second, third, fourth and fifth affirm loss of control and emphasize that such a person is no longer a human being. The phrase used "*Ame ma me ga le ame me o*," literally means "That person is no longer in a state of humanness," in other words he/she is "in a state of abnormalcy." This phrase was constantly used by most of the respondents during the interviews. The fourth informant also added that occasional drunkenness is not really alcoholism. This suggests that alcohol abusers are not true alcoholics even though one could progress from the former state to the latter. These responses suggest that alcoholism is a state where there is loss of control over one's drinking and one's thinking is distorted while normal functioning is curtailed.

What Are the Causes of Alcoholism?

When the respondents were asked to state what causes alcoholism, all affirmed spiritual causation. Others said it was due to deviant behaviour, socio-cultural influences and heredity. The following excerpts will substantiate this assertion:

First Informant: It could be a result of deviant behaviour which then progresses into this bad state. It could also be as a result of a curse or bewitchment.

Second Informant: It could be attributed to the commonality of alcohol in everyday life and activity (e.g. fishing, farming, community gatherings, etc). Though some may know that it is not good for them, they would drink so as not to be regarded as antisocial. We can then say that there are social and physical causes. However, we live in a world of not only the material but spiritual. I am a Christian but I believe in juju though I don't subscribe to it. People use juju, witchcraft, etc., to make others alcoholic due to envy, hatred, jealousy, etc. This is to make such afflicted persons useless or dysfunctional in society. This could be done directly or indirectly. A case in point is an only son of a wealthy man whose extended relatives did not want him to inherit the wealth of his father. Through spiritual means, they succeeded in making him an alcoholic, thus rendering him useless, irresponsible and therefore incapable of inheriting his father's wealth.

Third Informant: True alcoholism is through spirit possession. Some bring it from destiny (*se*). Others become alcoholics through the work of evil forces as a result of envy, bitterness, hurt, etc. It is thus not by their own volition to become alcoholics but as a result of friends/neighbours using some spirits of the air to attack them. Even though for some it is in their family or destiny(*se*), for many others and most common, are those which is the result of evil supernatural forces. These people are not born with it but because "a pot has been buried in their stomach (spiritually)," they continue to drink and just can't stay out of it.

Fourth Informant: First of all, alcoholism is caused by social groups, peer influence, customary and communal gatherings where drink is readily available. Some also become alcoholics through its continued use in their vocations/occupations like fishing, farming, etc. They drink to excite or encourage themselves in their work and to celebrate bumper catch/harvest. Frustrations that people go through during life crisis such as loss of job, death of spouse, a child or a significant other, etc., are also factors. In many other instances, the causes of alcoholism are spiritual. A story is told of a drunkard who had a personal god (*dzo*) and was insulted by someone as a useless being in society. The drunkard invoked a curse on the guy and he became a worse drunkard. Another story is told of a visit to the *Nogokpo* shrine. Here people are generally offered a drink. It is said that when one refuses the drink, even though one normally drinks alcohol, one would become a serious alcoholic. A curse from a previous generation can also indirectly manifest on succeeding members of a family.

Fifth Informant: First of all, I will say it is the result of deviant behaviour. It could also be caused by peer influence and also during a serious crisis such as loss of a parent or spouse. In such a situation, however, it is their own *"gblegble"* (deviant behaviour) or uncontrolled use that makes them alcoholics. I hate for people to wish evil on others. To seek evil for somebody is a great offence against God. When you offend the gods or the ancestors, evil will come upon you. That's why people will seek attachment to the sacred so they can be covered when evil attacks. Thus, supernatural causes are there but they are normally as a result of one's own actions and inactions against the gods, ancestors, etc. Some people may also wish you evil and consequently invoke the spirit of alcoholism on you.

Sixth Informant: First of all it is spiritual and could be deserved or underserved. In the situation of its being deserved, it means you are responsible or members of your family have wronged someone, the gods or the ancestors have breached some communal taboos. In the case of the undeserved it could be out of envy, etc. The consequences in these instances could also be either personal or corporate (involving family and generations). There are social causes too — peer pressure or a result of the nature of one's business, friends or family. There are those also said to be of destiny (*se-fenu*).

All of the informants mentioned supernatural or evil forces as causes of alcoholism. The first, second and fifth mention deviant behaviour which then progresses into an uncontrollable state. Socio-cultural causes were suggested by the second, fourth and sixth respondents and they suggested that peers, the commonality of alcohol in everyday life and activities are some of the main factors. The third and sixth defendants mentioned destiny, which is to say, such persons are born alcoholics thus emphasizing genetic, susceptibility, or the hereditary nature of alcohol addiction.

What Are the Effects of Alcoholism on the Family?

The following excerpts from the respondents point to the devastating effects of alcoholism on the family:

First Informant: It is enormous especially for the wife and children. First of all, it is economic. Then one's responsibility in the family as a whole is now in a vacuum, thus making one to become a burden on wife and children. It is also a disgrace to the family since the dignity of the individual and the family is lost due to the alcoholic's behaviour.

Second Informant: It affects families and destabilizes countries and society in general. One individual can make a difference for better or for worse. What positive impact can an alcoholic make? One becomes unproductive in the family, a burden for spouse, children and parents and ceases to be a role model for the community. People lose their honour and dignity due to the disgusting effects of alcoholism. There was a case of a teacher who was drunk and was smoking in class in front of his students. When he was called out, he fell headlong into a pool of water. The whole school saw him. It was so embarrassing that his children became subjects of ridicule in the school and community. They left the school. The whole person is a disgrace and it affects his family too.

Third Informant: It is a total disgrace to the family. The ladies get drunk and strip themselves naked. This is a total disgrace to womanhood. Husbands drink and abuse their wives and children; some even end up in police cells. They have become useless in the family. It is certainly true that some get involved due to stresses and certain unfortunate events in the family, but the negative consequences of alcohol only worsen their situations since more people are now affected by the individual's problems.

Fourth Informant: Once the man gets drunk, he loses control not only over himself but the entire family. Constant conflicts and even fights become the norm. The whole family is rendered dysfunctional due to the individual's dysfunction.

Fifth Informant: It is basically the individual's problem. Sometimes the problem is from the extended family. It is, however, the nuclear family that is mainly affected because there is always fighting and disharmony within the family. Don't worry my brother; this can be removed; *"agumaga"* reveals all the issues and restoration is done simply through rituals. If it is a curse that involves the whole family, the head of family or a significant person in the family is the one who goes through the ritual.

Sixth Informant: You have become dysfunctional in society, starting from your own immediate family. Your role as a member of the family is lost, thus rendering the family dysfunctional. Western society is individualistic but in Africa and for us, Ewes, we place emphasis on commonality. Everybody has a role to play and the individual is considered as one who contributes to the welfare of the group – entire households, the larger family, the clan and society at large. One's dysfunctionality is no longer an individual's problem but a corporate dysfunction. Also, the physical effects on one's health can affect others. Impotence, for example, cannot be said to be an individual's problem since when a young man is affected, wives are affected too.

All the respondents affirmed the negative consequences on the family as being shameful, disgraceful, involves loss of dignity and is unproductive to the family. Though the fifth informant responds "not really," he, however, asserted that the nuclear family is traumatized by the concomitant chaos that accompanies the individual's drinking in the home. Other ways the family is affected, as suggested by the respondents, include economic, physical and spiritual. The second and sixth respondents took it beyond one's immediate family to suggest that the community and society at large are also affected.

What Are the Traditional Modes of Curing the Alcoholic?

Most of the respondents gave cursory reflections on the traditional healing processes while the sixth informant gave a detailed description of the healing process.

First Informant: Traditionally, there are several processes, but I do not subscribe to them because within the traditional setting, once a person relapses, it becomes a curse and one's condition worsens. In the Christian setting, however, when one relapses, God's mercy is still available. For the Christian, first of all, one is taken through a process of counselling with support from scriptures on the negative effects and disastrous consequences of alcohol. It does not only destroy one's body but it destroys relationship with God, the church and others. Thereafter through much prayer, one is delivered and then rules are prescribed as guides to healthy spiritual life.

Second Informant: There are several modes of healing traditionally but most are spiritual-based. Traditionally, diviners have their own way of finding out what the causes are. If it is anything other than spiritual causation, some particular herbs are prescribed and one will never go near alcohol again. I once witnessed a case where the alcoholic was only given a piece of stick to chew on. Thereafter he was given some alcohol. He vomited so bad that he could no longer even stand the scent of alcohol. Whichever way, one's own willingness to overcome this problem is essential. Even with the material or physical causes, spiritual exorcism is done, even within the Christian context. Where there might be unwillingness, they still have a way of getting the alcoholic involved. Though some family members may not care about the individual's situation, the family is basically involved, especially the nuclear family. Some extended family members may not be so much concerned, and it only reflects the disunity or disharmony in the family. Where the cause has been identified as spiritual and to the extent that the whole family is involved, family heads take the lead in seeking restoration so as to bring peace and harmony within the entire family.

Third Informant: I know there are such healing practices but I am just a woman. I really don't know the process. I, however, know for certain that some rituals are performed and herbs are used to remove the alcoholic behaviour or spirit from the person.

Fourth Informant: Nowadays, I can talk about churches, herbalists and the shrines as healers. I met an old friend recently at a council meeting who said, "I was prayed for at a church and I quit drinking. Some time later, I tried a little and vomited everything." With the herbalists, there is a particular herb (a piece of stick) and once you chew on it, the smell of alcohol becomes very repulsive. These people will normally not tell you the name of the herbs. The priests and priestesses or diviners perform certain rituals after which you are cautioned and warned that a relapse will worsen the situation (which generally happens). Finally, I will say self-control is very important.

Fifth Informant: There are various levels of alcoholism. For those on a lower or milder level, we normally use herbs and counsel them. In more serious situations a lot of rituals are performed. First of all there is *"agumaga"* which is a process of consulting with the gods to find out the cause of the problem and seek guidance from *Mawu*. One is then taken through ritual bathing for seven days. Certain leaves (herbs) are used but there is a particular piece of stick which is very powerful in this regard and is given to the alcoholic to chew on. I can't tell you everything but it is all done under the guidance and direction of *Mawu*. If you want more, I have a friend at Anyako who is a specialist in this regard.

Sixth Informant: Traditionally there are certain rituals involved. First of all the diviners (*bokowo* — male diviners; *amegashie wo* — female diviners) go through a process of discovering the cause. This is known as *"agumaga"* (for the male diviners) or *"xoyoyo"* (for the female diviners). Generally this is a process of revealing the unknown. If they discover that it is a result of witchcraft or other evil forces, the process is then continued as follows:

- *Zameyi* or a visit to the night assembly of the witches to plead for the release of the head of the alcoholic or to get back the soul of the individual. When one is attacked, it is the "personality soul" (*luvɔ*) that is captured. Sacrifices are performed and the head of an animal is used to replace that of the individual. One of the animals is sacrificed in whole (holocaust) and no part is taken away. Sometimes the affliction is transferred in coins, etc., and anyone who picks it up, picks up the affliction on oneself. (The rationalist will explain this as a way of instilling moral discipline or as a form of social control). We must recognize, however, that everything in this worldview is very religious.

- Having performed this sacrifice, there is a ritual bath at night (*zalele*) after which certain prescriptions are made. These prescriptions generally involve things that are not to be done — sinful acts (taboos). Doing them means disobedience to the sacred. Such forbidden acts include food or drink.

- At this stage, drink is mixed with a herbal concoction, the smell of which is so repulsive that it takes away one's desire to drink. One is then made to drink this concoction.

- One then makes a vow to the *togbeɲɔliwo* (ancestral spirits), lesser gods and the Supreme Being not to drink again.

- Herbal mixture is then given to one to use in place of drink and this is not mixed with drink.

- This process is towards restoration and there should therefore be some willingness on the part of the alcoholic to go through the process. This is essential to begin the process. It is not done by proxy. Family members are encouraged to go through the process with the individual and rules are prescribed for them as well. This is to bring back life to one who has lost life, so the family cannot be left out. It is worth noting that there might be relapses but once there is progress, the process must be encouraged and facilitated.

Emphasis on spirituality and religion in the traditional healing process was mentioned by all the respondents. This affirms the mystical causation attributed to illness and problems in this worldview. They also assented to the use of herbalism as essential to this process. Though the first respondent said he did not subscribe to the traditional process, he however, did not reject its potency except for the fear that it encouraged alcoholics to avoid relapse. All respondents affirmed the importance of one's willingness and that of the family to go through the process.

It was also observed that while people were willing to go through the process, the traditional religious symbolisms or rituals also seemed to suggest paganism/fetishism which tended to put Christians away since it is viewed as contrary to Christian beliefs and practices. Also fear of serious repercussions if one should flout the vows could be a factor. However, the potency or effectiveness of the traditional healing methods cannot be over-emphasized. People's attitude, particularly family members, is one of concern while there seemed to be some aloofness on the part of the community. Is that to suggest that communal relations are breaking down? I suppose this could be due to the interpretations put on the alcoholic's behaviour. It is only in cases where there is a fear of repercussion on the community as a whole where one sees the community leaders taking the initiative to seek rehabilitation and restoration for the individual alcoholic as suggested by the fifth and sixth respondents.

What is the Ewe Concept of Health, Wholeness and the Cause of Illness?

First Informant: To be whole is simply to be a normal human being and be able to fulfill one's obligations to God and to society. Anything short of this means you have a problem, you are sick. Such infringements on life could be a result of sin, breach of taboos or diet, and negative behavioural practices such as womanizing, smoking and drinking. These generally tend to waste away life.

Second Informant: To talk about wholeness is to say the person is in a state of humanness; does things that will project a good image of oneself, family and society at large. A person is whole who is sober and upright in thought and could be consulted at anytime even if he/she is physically sick. Thus, to be whole or well-balanced as a human being is to be balanced or stable spiritually, relationally and physically. A lady nurse went to a funeral and got drunk. In an attempt to urinate, she took off her skirt, got entangled in it and fell flat on the ground and could not get up. It was a disgrace. This person has become less than a human being due to alcohol. I need not tell you that primarily among the Ewes, spiritual causes of illness cannot be overlooked. That is why people would go to the spiritualist and now churches for deliverance. Other causes of illness are basically our own actions and attitudes in relation to diet, etc. If I should assign portions, I would say causes of problems are two-thirds spiritual and one-third physical or material.

Third Informant: To be whole is to be well-balanced physically and spiritually. People can freely relate with you and you seek the well-being and happiness of others. Because you are spiritually strong, any evil planned against you will not succeed. Sicknesses and diseases are mainly from our relationship with the divine entities and also from our diet or bad eating habits.

Fourth Informant: It means to be well and in good health so as to be able to maintain oneself in the family and society. Some may be physically well but have no urge to do anything. Though they are not sick, they are out of balance. Basically they are emotionally or psychologically disturbed. Such a person cannot be said to be in a state of humanness or well-being. Others also may be physically ill and therefore not able to do anything or relate well. Such physical afflictions could be as a result of poor diet, unhealthy lifestyle, etc., and can be sorted out at the hospital. However, it is not all afflictions that can be handled at the hospital. Mystical causes, "*gbesa, dzo,*" etc., are spiritual means through which one could be rendered out of balance. These are not "hospital illnesses" but can only be healed through spiritual means.

Fifth Informant: To be precise, to be whole suggests someone who is in a state of humanness or who is a real person. One who is spiritually and physically strong and well-protected in all dimensions. Some bring afflictions upon themselves due to broken relationship with God and others. We are all human beings created by God but due to envy, jealousy and other negative relational tendencies, people seek to destroy others. People use the powers of their personal gods and witchcraft (*dzo, adze, tukpe,* etc.) to destroy others. Others also invoke the wrath of the gods and ancestors upon themselves through breach of taboos and neglecting of responsibilities to the gods and ancestors. There are also some afflictions that are hereditary and also those that we bring upon ourselves through diet, etc. In these instances, herbs are used to effect cure.

Sixth Informant: To be whole is to have a harmonious, peaceful and unifying relationship with God and others for the ultimate good of society or community as a going concern. To this end, there is no purely spiritual or physical affliction or wellness, though one cannot exist without the other. When two personality souls disagree with each other, it can lead to the destruction of your total well-being individually or corporately. In this worldview you don't heal diseases, you heal the whole person. For us the whole person involves the totality of the individual and is not separated from family or communal life. Healing therefore involves the totality of the person psychologically, socially, spiritually and physically. Psychological dysfunction can manifest in physical ailments. Thus broken relationships, etc., can manifest in physical symptoms.

Mystical or supernatural causes were mentioned by all the respondents. They emphasized breach of taboos, evil forces, curses, witchcraft, and also neglect of responsibilities to the gods and ancestors. Other sources of illness mentioned included poor diet, unhealthy lifestyle or negative behavioural patterns. Interestingly, all the respondents reflected on wholesome as being a "human being" or "to be in a state of humanness." Accordingly, they suggested that anything short of that must be sorted out. They also asserted that this is emphasized within the context of the family or community. For these respondents, being well-balanced in society involved spiritual, relational, psychological, social, and physical dimensions. This was summarized by the sixth respondent when he suggested that "in this worldview you don't heal diseases but you heal the whole person. Healing the whole person includes physical, spiritual, relational, and psychological, and it involves the totality of the person in relation to others and to God."

What is the Significance of Religion and Spirituality in this Context?

The important role of religion and spirituality was emphasized by all the respondents.

First Informant: Religion is very significant in this worldview and it is the way you relate to God that determines the way you function, normally or abnormally.

Second Informant: God is central in everything we do and God's power is needed to overcome any external force so as to be a proper human being. A relationship with the Supreme Being and any other source of power is therefore necessary. One must therefore abide by prescribed rules set by these powers so as not to incur their wrath.

Third Informant: The Christians say *Mawu*, we (traditional worshippers) also say *Mawu*. This is just to say *Mawu* is good and his presence is essential for our daily living. If you do well he will keep you well and keep you in a state of humanness but when you offend *Mawu* or the ancestors, or neglect your obligations to them, you will suffer for it.

Fourth Informant: Our beliefs are such that we can't forsake God in anything that we do. There are personal gods and community gods which basically function for our well-being. The stools are sacred and serve as a link between us and our ancestors who protect us and support us in times of need. However when we offend or break the rules prescribed to help us maintain harmony in life, we are severely punished for it. For example, women are not allowed to go to the stool house during menstruation. One of our chief's wives went in there and she went mad. Also, a man neglected to make the annual sacrifices to his personal god and after several years, he lost everything including a son and daughter under bizarre circumstances. When his negligence was later unfolded, the god was pacified through certain rituals of pacification and the strange events ceased.

Fifth Informant: We can't do anything without *Mawu Yehowa*. This fact is very important and must not be ignored in anyway. I begin my rituals with *Mawu* and end with *Mawu*. Once you call *Mawu* and then *torgbuiŋpliwo*, everything will be all right. They will be there for you. I believe that and I can't forget *Mawu*.

Sixth Informant: In this worldview, religion is indispensable. It is a sacred worldview. Human existence in this context is based on theocracy. In all ways, the gods of the family and the ancestors are regularly acknowledged and involved in everyday life.

Religion and spirituality is central worldwide. Its significance was emphasized by all the respondents throughout the interview. The centrality of the Supreme Being, ancestors and other spiritual forces was emphasized throughout the interview by all the respondents. This affirms that in this worldview the sacred and the secular are inseparable.

Interviews With Individual Alcoholics

Interviewing with individual alcoholics was intriguing. First of all, it was difficult identifying who a true alcoholic was. I therefore had to rely on the community elders to help identify some of them. I was aware that they might not readily admit their alcoholism due to the systemic denial often associated with it. However interviewing them was interesting as it gave me first-hand information about how alcoholics themselves felt about their situation. Four individuals were interviewed; male, female, young, old, married and unmarried. They were asked a general but open-ended question and this gave them the space to direct the interview. A reflection on their responses will help us understand how alcoholics feel about their situation.

First Respondent: I know people drink for several reasons; spousal problems, traumatic events and the most important is peer influence. I emphasize peer influence because I know I drink a lot, and in my case it's mainly peer influence. All my friends drink and for that matter we can't stay a moment without drinking. I know it's not good but how can I stop? What will my friends say? I need help. Alcohol is giving me a lot of problems. I am now very sick. I am at work now but I can't work. My wife and children are not happy. Anytime I get home drunk and my wife quarrels with me, I go out and drink more. It's like a cycle. Once I meet the guys, we just drink. As for the children, they don't tell me but I know they are not happy. They don't talk to me as I will want them to, but I know they are not happy. I am a Roman Catholic. I used to go to first mass but nowadays I don't. I can't drink and go to church. In fact, I am not happy. Alcohol gives me some satisfaction and is (it) the only consolation I have. How can I stay away from it? I wish I could stop but I can't. What will my friends say? I need help.

Second Respondent: My brother is it your problem? Nobody sends me to drink. What gives me happiness in life is what I do. The Bible does not forbid drinking but it forbids fornication. I don't fornicate. A lot of people are doing that. Their eyes are deceiving them — go and research that. Let me advise you, young man. Don't make anybody's problem your problem. Are you the one feeding my wife and children? Look, I have not lost my senses. I just went to "church" (to have a drink) this morning. Now I am fine. If I don't "pray" (drink), I can't do anything else. You can ask my wife. She just went out. She is a very beautiful woman and I don't give her problems. In life there are fools and there are stupid people and we have them in some families. As a man you have to try to be ahead of those people all the time. Seek satisfaction in life but don't make anybody's problem your problem. Are you a policeman? I am sure you don't drink. Do you smoke? (When I responded in the negative, he went on) *Ei!* then you will live long. Come back later let's talk. I want to be your friend. Alcohol is not a problem at all. I had been smoking cannabis before I joined the army at age 17. Now I don't smoke but for drink *ei!* It's my satisfaction.

Third Respondent: I don't know how it started but I can't live without it. I think it all started when my husband abandoned me accusing me of something I did not do. Little did I know that he was going to marry my friend. It was bad. He left all the children on me. He was actually a drunkard and I was taking care of the children before he left us. I was just taking it little by little and now I can't stop thinking about the fact that I can't stop drinking. As for my four children, they are all angry with their father but now I think they are angry with me too. They are all doing well. The two younger ones are living with relatives but they always come to see me. I gave them some education so the two adults are able to take care of themselves. One was living with me but we were always quarrelling so he moved out. But he always comes to see me. He just brought me from the hospital. I know they are now ashamed but I am ashamed too. They are worried and I am worried too but there is nothing I can do. I will just die and that will end it all. I drink but I don't misbehave like some women do. So mine is better. I don't want to embarrass anybody.

Fourth Respondent: Everybody is upset with me because I drink. My sisters are upset and sometimes I feel like they wish I was not their brother. As for my parents, I know they are worried. They may have their own problems but now I can feel it by the way they look at me and relate with me. Sometimes I am fine but at other times, I just can't stop. I need it every moment to be able to function. It is from dawn to dusk. I try to stop but the pain is too much. I become so restless, I have to take some more to be fine. My problem is very spiritual. I can't go to church anymore. I hear my younger sisters left our church to join another church because they say I am embarrassing them. Well, I don't know. My elder sister is so worried I hear she is not eating. She was admitted at the hospital last week. We live in the same house but nobody told me. Am I so useless? I will make it with the help of God. I will come and see you later and we can talk more.

From the responses, though three admitted their loss of control over alcohol, one, I can say, was still in a state of denial and did not think his drinking behaviour was a problem to anybody. The three admitted they were alcoholics and their drinking affects their families in many ways including spiritually. Other effects mentioned included shame and disgrace, quarrels, broken relationships or disharmony. The first respondent mentioned peer influence or social drinking as the cause of his alcoholism. Blaming peers for one's alcoholism is noted as a common way for alcoholics dealing with their drinking. The second respondent, however, uses the tactic of diverting attention from the self by generalizing and saying "a lot of people are doing it." The implication of this statement is that it might be okay. One therefore sees a lot of defensiveness and denial that shows up in the response. The third respondent mentioned a crisis in life from which her drinking progressed to this uncontrollable state. She is, however, *projecting* her drinking on her husband. Certainly, that can precipitate drinking though it is worth emphasizing that a lot of husbands leave their wives yet they do not resort to drinking. One clearly sees the issue of shame clearly reflected in her response, though she also plays a game of *comparison*. "I may be ashamed of my drinking, but at least I am not as bad as some women who misbehave!" Knowing that the family is embarrassed by what is happening, she therefore resorts to using *withdrawal* as a mechanism to deal with the "shame" and the sense of lack of control.

All three respondents affirmed mystical causality when they said their problem could be spiritual. They affirmed its effects on them physically and relationally and their need for help. Feelings of helplessness, despair and anguish were reflected by the alcoholics throughout the interviews. This suggests their state of confusion and despair. Though there were occasional reflections of pride, in that they do not understand why people were so much concerned about them, the guilt, remorse, shame and self hatred accompanying their alcoholism could be attributed to their self-esteem having sunk low. This caused them to withdraw more into their inner world, alienated from others. Consequently, feelings of loneliness and discouragement were fostered.

Interviews With Family Members

I now present some of the interviews with family members by giving a summary of their responses to the question: *How does the individual's alcoholism affect you and the family?* I also present one case which was a group interview in verbatim form.

First Respondent: He is of no use, no reward to the family. We are poor folks but he has no idea what goes on around him, whether good or bad. They are men, and are supposed to lead the family in taking decisions and we ladies have been left as orphans. I don't know why he drinks (*sobbing*). He is not married and has no child. He is impotent. But I don't think that is the problem. His late senior brother, a good fisherman, was also an alcoholic but he had children, and so is our junior brother in Accra. Our late brother's children and grandchildren in Togo are all drunkards now. The whole family is destroyed. Drink has become everything to the guys. It is terrible and we can't help it. Honestly, we don't even want to talk about it. He is now very sick. Through traditional means he was healed and warned not to try it again but he did not obey instructions. Now he is worse, a total embarrassment. We hear our father, a chief fisherman in his time was an alcoholic but in his case it was spiritual. Some people used *juju* on him out of envy. Some think that is what is affecting the guys now through the generations. I don't know. In fact, it is not good to have an alcoholic in the family. It destroys the whole family (*sobbing*).

Second Respondent: As for my husband, I know people drink but for him, I don't know why he drinks. Honestly, there is no peace in the house. We are always quarrelling. If I am the cause of his problems he should let me know and I will leave. But look at him, how can I leave him? Who will care for him? What would people say? In fact, I need my husband. The children need him too and I know whatever spirits are controlling him will certainly leave him in Jesus' name. Yesterday, he said I was a witch. Today he said he will kill me. How can I live with this man who has no respect for us? He does not know when the children wake up or when they go to sleep. As for their school fees he pays and he provides for the home. But when he drinks, he is a different person. The children don't want him to come to their school because they say their friends will laugh at them. What kind of disgrace is this? In fact, we need him. I am married but for about six years now, I don't have a husband (*sobbing*) why? I pray God will have mercy on us so he can also change.

Third Respondent: This boy is killing me. I have done all I could for him. Now I hear he smokes Indian hemp as well. Why should God allow this to happen to me? I am an educationist and highly respected woman at church. Look at my son—total embarrassment. If it is anything that I have done wrong, I pray God should have mercy and forgive me. Now look at me. There are certain places I have to be careful what I say. I now have to constantly monitor my blood pressure, *hmm*!! (*Long pause*) In fact, the stress is too much. Why me? The worst part is he doesn't think he has a problem. Then stop? He is always drunk and because of that his appointment cannot be confirmed at work. He is still a casual worker. How could he continue at this age?

Fourth Respondent: My brother is an alcoholic. The truth is, now he is hopeless. He is the eldest but now I have to care for his children. Our mother was doing it but now she is very sick so it's all my responsibility now. I am not in town but he doesn't care about our mother. He is always with his friends drinking. If our father were alive, I wonder what he would have done. Can we talk about something else? The pain is too much for me. I can't stand him. He has destroyed our family. In fact, my brother, I don't want to talk about this issue.

Group Interview

This is an extract of an interview with an alcoholic family. (The alcoholic was with her mother, sister and son.)

Researcher (R.1):   How are you doing and how is my sister's alcoholism affecting you as a family?

Mother   (M.1):   *Hmm*!! She is here. Let her speak for herself.

Alcoholic   (A.1):   I don't know what's going on. I have been living with my husband and kids in Abidjan and all of a sudden I just got into this situation and I still can't understand. Sometimes I seem to be well but at other times I feel so restless. I have had some physical afflictions that set me thinking a lot and it's stressful. My mother and the whole family are worried about me. But it's not my fault. I don't want to drink but it looks like some forces are driving me to. I have been having some nightmares and it's not that I just get up to drink. Everybody is worried. I sew for people they don't want to pay me.

(M.2):   She was doing very well. Very educated and even taught in a school for a while. Remarried and travelled with the second husband to Abidjan where they were brewing local gin. The man started complaining of her drinking habits and beat her. We asked the man to bring her back

home to us and she's not been well since. She's been sick several times, had many ailments and has been in out of the hospital several times with the support of her siblings. Now that she's saying it's spiritual, God help us, otherwise I don't understand why with all the efforts she can't quit. It is destroying the family. There is disharmony; nobody wants to send her money. I am the one who is always trying to do what I have to do. Been to several places myself but now I don't have money. The siblings don't want to support me in that regard. They are Christians and they say she should go to church and pray and she would be fine. I don't have money, they are the ones feeding me and they are not willing for their money to go to where I could take her, so what can I do?

Sister (S.1): She was the one who introduced me to the Christian faith but now she doesn't even know the door of the church. Now see. Sometime ago it's on and off. When she is with us sometimes she's fine. When she leaves to go back to her house, she then becomes something else — now honestly there is nothing I can do — it's her problem — now all our siblings have given up on her — so let her do what she wants to do — drink to death — we would bury her.

(R.2): Sister, I hear your pain and I know how it feels like. Do I hear you saying you don't care what happens to your sister?

(S.2): (*Sobbing*) We are all trying because her condition is troubling all of us. We are all restless, but for how long can we keep our focus on her? She now hates the church.

Why can't she pray for herself? Why can't she control herself? We are all tired. *(At this point, a young man sitting with us, whom I later found out to be the son of the alcoholic left us abruptly.)*

(M.3):   I brought her forth, now my child is doing this — a shame to my motherhood and nobody seems to care now — here I am thinking what to do. We know it can be healed traditionally but I don't have the money — the siblings say they are Christians and that she should go to church and be healed. *(Pause)* I have been living with it since 1993.

(R.3):   Do you have other children? How are they taking this?

(A.2):   I have five children but they are all living with relatives out of town. I know they are all ashamed of this but what can I do?

(M.4):   The youngest one is always insulting her. Her second son (but third child) is the one who was sitting here and you see the way he just left. You can tell he isn't happy.

(A.3):   As for that girl she doesn't respect her elders. I may be horrible but she does not respect. The others are not with me. We don't talk much but I pray to God for them. I hear they are fine.

All the respondents characterize their alcoholic relatives as useless, unproductive and an embarrassment to the family. One significant observation was that it was very stressful for them talking about the issues. Among the family respondents, the issue of "shame" is very paramount. In the case of the second respondent, one notes the woman showing strong indications of "codependency," which suggests that those "affected" can get just as sick as those "afflicted." This is because they try to control the drinking; and their lives are built around the one drinking.

The first and second respondents were even sobbing intermittently and one could thus feel the pain underlying their responses as they tried to talk about the issues. The second and third respondents reflected guilt feelings and asked if they were the problem which might suggest that the alcoholic is just an identified patient or symptomatic carrier of whatever problems might be inherent within the system. In the case of the first respondent the implication of hereditary or genetic transmission as influencing alcoholism within the family cannot be ruled out. In all situations, however, spiritual causality was suggested.

Apart from the first respondent who said they once sought traditional healing for the individual alcoholic, the others, though were aware of its availability even in the Christian setting, seem to be waiting for help to come to them. This could probably be the situation due to their feelings of hopelessness and helplessness that characterize their alcoholic situation which, as suggested earlier, is associated with shame and the conspiracy of silence.

During the group interview, it was also observed that though the mother realized that help was readily available in the traditional religious context, the children who are Christians were not willing to support her to go through the process. They, however, thought the alcoholic should pray and would be fine, forgetting that this was a spiritual disease and the alcoholic "cannot function with ease in relation to God, just as the physical disease of alcoholism is that one cannot function with ease in relation to alcohol."[339] Such a response which is typical of Christians is so naive and simplistic, thus calling for serious education for people about the realities of addiction.

Discussion

Reflections on the results suggest that alcoholism is a real and present danger in the family among the Ewes of southeastern

---

[339] Royce, *Alcohol and Other Drug*, p. 514.

Ghana. It also suggests that any meaningful quest for healing must be wholistic and complete; psychologically, physiologically, and spiritually, and must be integrative, encompassing the family. This is more so since the social context within which the person abides and interacts is relevant to understanding one's experiences. Boisen posited that meanings can be derived from people's experiences and it is these experiences that reflect one's theological conceptions. I will therefore attempt to dialogically interpret and give meaning to the condition of the alcoholic and his/her family, based on the belief that the problem of the troubled individual and the family is the inability to give meaning to their experiences and ideas. This will help us understand the Ewes' conception of alcoholism in general and how it involves the family.

The Ewe understanding or conception of an alcoholic suggests one who has lost control over his/her drinking and is out of balance spiritually, socially, economically, physically and psychologically. According to some of the informants:

Second Informant: In short, alcohol takes a better part of the person, puts him out of balance and therefore cannot think or act properly. Drink becomes a basic need for such a person without which life will be impossible.

Sixth Informant: It means using alcohol in a way that makes you unproductive. To such a person alcohol is now the key to wholeness. One cannot do without it.

This Ewe view seems to be concomitant with the general description of alcoholism as reflected on earlier in this chapter. Thus, though socio-cultural contexts define one's view of alcohol, meanings as in this case could also be general. Clinebell asserts that the behaviour characteristics of the illness are "craving for the psycho-physiological effects of alcohol and continuing excessive use of alcoholic beverages in ways that are harmful to the user and many others . . . and often results in grave physiological and psychiatric complications."[340] From the foregoing, one recognizes that the Ewe understanding of

---

[340] Clinebell, *Understanding and Counselling*, p. 23.

alcoholism can best be described more within the context of its effects on the person and others. This emphasizes psycho-social and relational rather than physiological, though it is not denied. This can be further understood as we reflect on the Ewe suppositions of what the causes generally are.

Socio-cultural and spiritual causation have been emphasized as primary. Due to its commonality in everyday life and activity, alcohol abuse, which could easily progress to the addiction phase, is very common, thus characterizing it as being a result of deviant behaviour. This process, according to the third and sixth respondents, is however not as grave as the spiritual causation cases. True alcoholism could herein be defined as being a result of supernatural forces such as witchcraft, offending the gods and others. Thus, broken relationships between humans and humans, and between humans and the spirit world are significant factors that influence alcoholism. This is to suggest that though social and environmental factors account for alcoholism among the Ewe, mystical causation is of extreme significance and must not be overlooked. Again the third and sixth respondents suggest "destiny" (*Se or Sefenu*). This indicates that genetic transmission or heredity is a considerable cause of alcoholism in this regard.[341]

Consequently, one recognizes that to meaningfully reflect on alcoholism in this milieu, it is very necessary not to consider these causation factors in isolation. The "wholistic" model, as emphasized earlier, is therefore very relevant to this worldview as one seeks to understand the nature and influencing factors of alcoholism. Generally, in this milieu, though physical and mystical causation of illness is emphasized, the sacred overshadows the secular and physical explanations are often sought within the framework of the supernatural and within the context of one's relations. This supposition is true for alcoholism too. From the above, the Ewe would therefore probably restate ASAM's 1990 definition of alcoholism to suggest that:

Alcoholism is a primary chronic spiritual disease with spiritual, psycho-social, environmental and genetic factors influencing its development and manifestation. It is

---

[341] See D.W. Goodwin. *Is Alcoholism Hereditary?* Oxford University Press, 1976.

progressive and fatal and characterized by continuous impaired control over drinking, preoccupation with the drug alcohol, use of alcohol despite adverse consequences which invariably keeps one out of balance, breaks down family and other relationships, and distortions in thinking, mostly denial. It primarily takes one out of a state of 'humanness.'

It has been affirmed that the presence of alcoholism in the family is of grave consequence, especially to the wife and children. Aside from the economic, physical, and social effects as well as the general state of disharmony that engulfs the family, shame and disgrace seem to be emphasized by all the respondents. As an effect, emotion or feeling, Hunsinger agrees with Gershen Kaufman in suggesting that, feelings of shame are tantamount to being seen as basically deficient in some fundamental aspect of being human, and this is accompanied by a feeling of powerlessness. For Kaufman, this is an impotent making experience which puts the alcoholic and his/her family out of balance.

Dysfunctional families of alcoholics are generally said to be confronted with feelings of shame, guilt, fear, anger, emptiness, loneliness, worthlessness, helplessness and hopelessness. These feelings are influenced by a set of defence mechanisms notably denial, which tend to leave the alcoholic and his/her family in a systemic scheme of silence and isolation. Also since children get their worth from parents and significant others, in cases where alcoholism is used to sedate pain, these perceptions are learned by the children and the family's dysfunctionality tends to be in perpetuity. It is in trying to cover up this debilitating situation of codependency that families get caught up in the deadly conspiracy to be silent. This conspiracy could also account for why members of the nuclear family will tend to keep their individual alcoholic's situation away from other members of the extended family so as to avoid being shamed. It was interesting to hear some of the responses on the concomitant physical effects on members of the family. Albers notes that such psychosomatic effects manifest in so many forms on the health of family members.[342]

---

[342] Albers, *Shame and the Conspiracy of Silence*, p. 58.

Apart from spiritual causation that may get the attention of even the extended family and community, those cases that are viewed as being a result of deviant behaviour are often seen as the individual's problem. It is therefore expected of the individual to be able to exercise control. This is unfortunate. Royce contends that "since the drinking of alcoholics is not a matter of choice but the symptom of a disease, there is no use in appealing to good will or exhorting them to use will power. That is like telling the tubercular patient not to cough."[343] For Spickard and Thompson, "strong determination is no defense against addiction."[344] Thus, appealing to will power is an improbable task. Also, if genetic susceptibility is a factor in the addiction process, then the vulnerability of generations to come is at risk. This generally leaves the family and the alcoholic in a hopeless situation craving for meaning and value in life. An assurance of faith in a higher power as being able to empower oneself to overcome the weaknesses of alcohol is therefore necessary for any meaningful recovery process.

Nukunya suggests that there is little doubt that the traditional practices and institutions described in earlier chapters are no more operational with the same force and intensity. Western education, Christianity and urbanization are some of the factors that have sought to influence our tradition.[345] It should be remembered that missionary, Christianity is opposed, in many ways, to traditional life and the fact that religion relates to other aspects of the social life of the Ewes suggests that these related institutions, including the family, are also affected.[346] "The missionaries opposed not only religious practices but also anything traditional or African and considered them pagan."[347] Focus therefore sought to shift more to "families of procreation and less on those of orientation and the extended family as a whole."[348] This view of some of the respondents, however,

---

[343] Royce, *Alcohol and Other Drug*, p. 312.

[344] Spickard and Thompson, *Dying for a Drink*, p. 39.

[345] Nukunya, *Tradition and Change: An Introduction*, p. 138.

[346] See Mercy A. Oduyoye. *Hearing and Knowing: Theological Reflections on Christianity in Africa*. Maryknoll, NY: Orbis Books, 1986.

[347] Nukunya, *Tradition and Change*, p. 122.

[348] Nukunya, *Tradition and Change*, p. 135.

cannot be said to be the general view of the people, since most of them have persistently emphasized the relevance of the family in any meaningful therapeutic process.

Despite these forces of change on the traditional society, the impact of alcoholism on the family, according to the respondents, is of intense concern to the family members and the community at large. This suggests that the power of the community and relations is still very relevant in this milieu. One informant said of an alcoholic, "If she goes out, somebody would ask of her 'Which house are you from?' She might not be of herself because of the drink but the name of the entire family and community is stigmatized." Families will therefore do anything possible to resolve such issues that tend to put the family out of balance and work towards maintaining relational harmony.

It will therefore not be erroneous to conclude from these reflections that despite the influence of westernization, Christianity and urbanization on the traditional society, the family is still a force within which context values, attitudes and behaviour of the individual is defined. Generally, it has been acknowledged that anything that affects the individual invariably destabilizes the family's equilibrium. Since the family is one significant context within which the ritual and social use of alcohol is emphasized in relation to alcohol-related problems, members of the family thus aim at behaviours and practices toward maintaining a homeostatic balance. A meaningful change in the system towards wholeness must therefore consider the family as a system due most importantly to the relationality and communality of the Ewe family. An informant affirms thus:

> Western society is individualistic but in Africa and for us Ewes, corporate emphasis is essential . . . One's dysfunctionality is no longer an individual's problem but a corporate dysfunctionality.[349]

Gaba suggests that alcoholism in the family fosters disharmony hence dysfunctionality within the family and

---

[349] See Sixth Informant's response to question three of key informants' interview.

community. "Where there is disharmony, the family and society tend to dysfunction or disintegrate and growth or homeostatic balance is not attained." It is to this goal of maintaining relational harmony that Ewe practices such as *nugbidodo* is aimed at restoring harmony for broken relationships within the family and community at large, embracing both the living and the dead.[350] This supposition basically affirms the systemic nature of the African family where the problem of an individual as well as his/her restoration cannot be considered in isolation of other members of the family since the individual's problem may just be a symptom or manifestation of the general problems inherent within the family. Thus, the individual is just a symptomatic carrier (identified patient) of the general problems within the family.

It has been suggested that due to the interconnections within the family system, any change in the individual reverberates through the entire system while family members also change in order to keep the system in balance. Denial is used as a defence so as to maintain the stability of the family system in the face of environmental and developmental stresses. This is, however, unhealthy since what is needed for learning and growth to occur is change in the system. When this is done meaningfully, the entire system is encouraged to help solve one another's problems and not cut off from the life-enhancing enrichment of the social milieu.

According to Cosgrove and Hatfield, even though family systems tend towards homeostasis, they can also adapt to pressure from change within or outside the system by restructuring themselves. This is because the psychic life of the individual is not only private but also social and any consistent change in the behaviour of a family member evokes a considerable change elsewhere in the system.[351] To therefore foster change and enhance growth and family cohesion, Masamba ma Mpolo writes:

The extended family re-invents itself by using its inherent capacity to be the center par excellence of support for, and

---

350 Gaba, interview.
351 Charles H. Cosgrove and Dennis D. Hatfield. *Church Conflicts: The Hidden Systems Behind the Fights.* Nashville: Abingdon Press, 1994, p. 124f.

confrontation among its members, thus enabling the individual as well as the entire family, through dialogue and rituals of reconciliation, to deal constructively with conflicting and inhibiting personal drives, cultural and religious values. This family arrangement creates psychosocial atmosphere conducive to personal growth and family cohesion.[352]

Even though family systems thinking is so well developed in western cultures despite the individualistic nature of this society, the fact that it is not so well developed in the African milieu should not suggest its irrelevancy. The nature, dynamics and functions of the African family clearly reflect the true nature of family systems thinking in general, and the multigenerational family systems thinking in particular, even more than in western society. As discussed earlier, the individual family member cannot be defined or identified in isolation from the family of origin or lineage from which one derives. It has also been noted from the above reflections that one's dysfunctional behaviour invariably breeds disharmony in the family while family stresses and traumas consistently manifest in several forms of dysfunctionality, including alcoholism, in the individual and in generations to come. Since the alcoholic family's dysfunctionality and shame is fostered through the severing of the interpersonal bridge, meaningful restoration can begin through the restoration of the interpersonal bridge so as to maintain relational harmony. Relational harmony can be maintained only within the context of mutual love. Thus, through an assurance of love within the context of meaningful relations, restoration for the family and the individual can be meaningfully attained.

Traditional healing modes are noted as very effective and aimed at "restoring life to one who has lost life."[353] It involves restoration of broken relationships and appeasement of the ancestors and gods, where they were offended. In cases of evil forces, such restoration involves redeeming of the head or soul

---

[352] Masamba ma Mpolo. "Perspectives on African Pastoral Counselling," in *The Risks of Growth: Counselling and Pastoral Theology in the African Context* (World Council of Churches, 1985) p.2.

[353] Gaba, interview.

of the alcoholic. Though herbs are used, the religious rituals attached reflect the emphasis this worldview places on mystical causality. The effectiveness of the traditional healing process, as suggested by the respondents, can be described as a very potent veracity which is very much upheld by the community. However, two issues reflected by the respondents call for attention as one considers the similarities and dissimilarities in the Christian and traditional approaches to healing and its implication for the Ghanaian Christian.

First of all the fear of repercussions, not only on the individual but the family, in cases of relapse, tends to hold people back from taking advantage of the traditional process though they do not negate its efficacy. Secondly, because of the religious implications involved animal sacrifice, ritual bath and herbalism, Christians tend to avoid the traditional processes so as not to be seen as indulging in heathen practices. This particular situation can be reflected on in terms of westernization or the impact of missionary Christianity on the African worldview.

Ghunney agrees with Nukunya in suggesting that Christianity and westernization of the African has affected African forms of medicine.[354] Furthermore, Twumasi, just like Bonsi and Senah, also proposes that usually, both educated and uneducated adherents do not admit that they use traditional healing agencies. This could be due to the teachings of Christianity which condemn traditional healing practices. Hence, "some of the old structures which gave credence to traditional medical theory are breaking down in the face of the new changes which have come about."[355]

As one reflects on the first issue, one is confronted with the high regard this worldview holds of the sacred. Since it has been affirmed that a high level of powerlessness over alcohol influences alcoholism and submission to a higher power leads to restoration, it will therefore not be erroneous to propose that this reverence of the sacred and also fear of repercussions should rather be redirected and reflected on as a loving force influencing people to seek healing and consequently adhering to whatever prescriptions that might be set. Fear in this context is not fear of

---

[354] Ghunney, *African Spiritual Worldview*, p. 112f.
[355] E.A. Twumasi. *Medical Systems in Ghana*. Accra: Ghana Publishing Co., 1975 p. 101, 110.

the sacred, but rather fear of the consequences that might befall one if they flout the rules set to guide their recovery.

It has also been affirmed that missionary churches, like the Pentecostal/Charismatic churches, in this locality and for that matter the whole of Ghana, generally use healing practices that are appealing to the indigenous people. Such practices are probably more appealing since they point to mystical causes for problems and diseases. Thus, its relevance within the context of this worldview must be continuously emphasized so as to appeal to Christianity for answers to existential questions of "Why am I suffering this affliction?" and "Who or what is responsible for this illness?" It has been suggested that the African is fundamentally seeking access to spiritual power that can help him/her to overcome the forces that disrupt life. Thus, any move towards accessing such power would be appealing to the African Christian family as it seeks restoration for itself.

The therapeutic process in these churches is multi-dimensional and is made up of a spiritual prognosis followed by a prescribed procedure of healing which may include rituals of deliverance of various forms. This is aimed at exorcising the evil or supernatural force behind one's ailment. At the Grace Presbyterian Healing Centre, Akropong, it was noted that though they acknowledged the causes of alcoholism as being possibly social, psychological, and spiritual, Dr. Dankwa notes that "the general health condition and psychological impairments can also be reversed in the same way as the spiritual causes which are generally a result of curses, wrongdoing, projection by witchcraft, family covenant, etc."[356]

In the healing process, there is first of all an interaction with the alcoholic and any family member present. Subsequently, a prayer session is held so as to find the cause or source of the individual's affliction. A prayer line, which is a series of prayerful affirmations based on scripture, is then given to the client to go through. This is to help build one's faith and enable one to recognize his/her powerlessness over alcohol. It is also to move the alcohol addict from a state of denial to accept the reality of

---

[356] Interview with Dr. Dankwa, a plant pathologist and now a prayer warrior in charge of alcoholism problems at Grace Presbyterian Healing Centre, Akropong, Akwapim, on 17 April, 2004.

one's situation so as to be able to deny oneself of alcohol. One is then taken through a deliverance session where one is exorcised of the forces behind one's affliction. In the case of family covenant, a process of "family deliverance" is initiated. Thereafter, a set of rules are prescribed and the "delivered" alcoholic is now helped to channel his/her energy into something productive, such as crop farming and animal rearing.

Reflecting on the responses from the respondents coupled with other information gathered in this study, it is worth agreeing with Akrong when he surmises that the therapeutic process of these churches is made up of what might be described as multi-dimensional levels of therapies, which allow the particular spiritual agent who is the source of the illness to be overcome on the spiritual plane through the power of Jesus, the Holy Spirit or an angel. Church rituals aimed at exorcising an evil spirit or cleansing the patient from evil contamination that may account for the illness, have great affinities with traditional therapeutic systems. Other procedures such as prognosis process, verbal therapy, ritual cleansing, rituals of touch, ritual of exorcism and care by relatives and family, clearly show a creative synthesis of traditional and Christian theological ideas woven into Ghanaian Christian healing procedures.[357]

From this research therefore, the reality of alcoholism as a clear and present danger that engulfs families cannot be overemphasized. It destabilizes families and renders the individual impotent as a "human being" while rendering the entire family dysfunctional. Though in some instances, the extended family due to the impact of social change may be seen as aloof in matters concerning the alcoholic, its importance in stabilizing the family and seeking restoration and well-being for its individual members cannot be overlooked. Healing is therefore aimed at restoration of not only the individual into a state of "humanness" but also the family into a state of harmony. I suppose this is what Masamba ma Mpolo suggests when he states:

> The restoration of broken relationships, the re-establishment of social equilibrium, the re-vitalization of individual

---

[357] Akrong, *African Religious, Media and Health*, p. 6-7.

identity within the context of the renewed community are all major means and dynamic ends underlying traditional therapies and healing processes.[358]

Renewed community in this case cannot refer to a family in its state of disequilibrium or dysfunctionality, but a family that has also experienced or is experiencing significant healing for its afflictions. Thus, as healing is sought for the family's stresses and traumas, the individual's stabilization within the system is assured. It is within the context of this renewed community that a trusted loving community can best be experienced.

With the emphasis by the informants or respondents on mystical causality as influencing alcoholism coupled with its degradations or stigmatizing effects on the family, any meaningful quest for restoring the alcoholic to a state of "humanness" or wholeness must therefore be integrative and must involve the family towards a wholistic recovery. Here, the individual is restored in the midst of a dynamic balance in the family and within the larger social system, including ancestors and spirit beings. We can herein surmise that the traditional therapeutic processes as well as the healing processes of the churches seek to stimulate faith and the restoration of hope for the alcoholic and his or her family within loving relationships.

Generally, the systemic worldview of the Ewes reflects a people who are relational with a keen sense of communality. It is a sacred worldview and relationships are emphasized within the purview of the sacred. Reflections on wholeness have persistently emphasized relational wellness in the light of what God has ordained humankind to be. Whatever mode of therapy, it must therefore be integrative and aimed at restoring the alcoholic into a state of humanness, becoming who God has created one to be. This process of restoration is tantamount to restoring life to one who has lost it. It must therefore seek to help the alcoholic and his/her family towards attaining freedom in God and from the bondage of alcoholism.

To this end, it is essential to emphasize that from the

---

[358] Masamba ma Mpolo, *Perspectives*, p. 10.

foregoing discussion, any meaningful quest for wholeness must embrace the family so as to lead to a dynamic balance. Spirituality, though very paramount in this search for healing, must be employed within the context of the family so as to lead to a holistic wellness. Those significant others who are adversely affected and are involved with alcoholism, need healing even more than the individual alcoholic. Robert Albers was noted to have said of a friend who often made a bold and shocking statement, "Forget about the one who is suffering from the disease, and work in your ministry with those significant others who are affected."[359] It must be emphasized that spirituality as emphasized in this context is one of relationship not of isolation. It is one that seeks to lead the individual alcoholic and his/her family to admit their powerlessness over alcohol and seek God's grace for their broken lives. This is a spirituality that acknowledges human suffering and weakness and seeks healing for one's afflictions. Such a spirituality that seeks a trusted loving higher power and a trusted loving human community is one that invariably seeks to propel both the afflicted and the numerous others who are adversely affected towards a state of "humanness." Thus, it is only when weaknesses in the system are acknowledged and brought to light that restoration can be meaningful and complete.

Whether viewed as sin from the moral point of view or as an illness from which one needs to be cured, the above reflections suggest that the alcoholic has become something other than he/she was created to be; something other than human. This suggests that the person's ability to become all that he/she was created to be as a human being is compromised. One's capabilities has significantly been diminished due to the ensnaring and enslaving effects of alcoholism. Thus, one has lost the freedom to live as one created in God's own image.

According to Nukunya, to be in a state of "humanness" suggests "well-being or being healthy in all dimensions. It is not limited to the absence of disease but includes relational, moral, spiritual, physical and psychological uprightness. It connotes a major state of well-being and reflects a person who could be

---

[359] Albers, *Continuity and Change*, p. 4.

easily approached and who could go about his/her normal functioning without interruption."[360] This state of humanness is what is basically reflected in the biblical concepts of *shalom* and *soteria*. Thus, if one has lost this state, it clearly suggests that one's relationship with oneself, others, the environment and with God is jeopardized. One's freedom to live is thereby curtailed.

According to Daniel Migliore, in *Faith Seeking Understanding: An Introduction to Christian Theology*, to be in such a negative state of humanness where hopelessness, loneliness, helplessness, worthlessness, guilt, and shame are the norm, indicates that one by this condition has lost the freedom to live. Migliore calls this freedom the "created freedom" and goes further to enumerate its dimensions as:

> Relationship to and responsibility before God, life in relationship with others, and openness to God's promise . . . Our created freedom is awakened by God's address to us, expanded by our co-existence with others very different from us, and directed toward a future fulfillment in the coming reign of God.[361]

When such a relationship is lost, one's freedom is endangered. One will therefore need to be delivered so as to be able to participate in a new humanity in Christ Jesus. It is this kind of restoration that traditional therapeutic processes seem to emphasize and which is relevant for the restoration of the alcoholic and his/her family. This state of humanness is realized to its fullness as reflected in *shalom*. Consequently, it is worth emphasizing that the ministry of Jesus is a picture of what it means to be truly and fully human.

For Migliore therefore, participation in this new humanity with Jesus Christ is what is objectified in the Christian concepts of *faith*, *love* and *hope*. Being human connotes being called to

---

[360] Interview with Professor G.K. Nukunya at the Department of Sociology, University of Ghana on 5 June, 2007.
[361] Daniel Migliore. *Faith Seeking Understanding: An Introduction to Christian Theology*, Second Edition (Grand Rapids: Michigan: W.B. Eerdmans Publishing Co., 2004) p. 160-162.

participate in, and in some sense reflect God's own life of relationship and communion. In this case, Christian freedom connotes freedom *from* the bondage of alcohol or anything that seeks to take life away, *for* partnership with God and others. The foundation for this state lies not in oneself but lies in the "forgiving grace of God present in the new humanity of Jesus with whom we are united by the power of the Holy Spirit."[362] This is the perfect realization of being human in undistorted relationship with God. Thus, due to the loss of created freedom of the alcoholic and the family coupled with their resultant loss of the worth of their humanity through alienation from God and others, restoration to wholeness (*shalom*) comes through total surrender to a "Higher Power," God, and participation by faith, love, and hope in the new humanity present in Jesus the Christ. This must certainly be total and not partial, involving the family and not the individual in isolation, for it to be healthy and helpful.

---

[362] Migliore, *Faith Seeking Understanding*, p. 160.

5

Final Words

In writing the conclusion to this study and proposing a "wholistic" healing model, it will be relevant to consider the implications of this study for pastoral care and counselling as well as for the Church. Since this work also seeks to serve as an impetus for further research, it is expected to stimulate further thinking in the area of alcohol addiction in the African context as I also make some recommendations for further study.

The great Roman philosopher, Seneca, referred to alcoholism as a form of insanity. Some refer to it as a physiological or psychosomatic illness.[378] For some it is a psychological illness, accordingly suggesting a mental defect, while to others it is hereditary in nature. Though some refer to it as a matter of public health of the first order,[379] we have sought to assert in this study that alcoholism is a social, economic, physiological, psychological, legal and a spiritual problem whose effects are overwhelming, enormous, and devastating for the family.

The menacing, all-encompassing and chronic nature of alcoholism causes the Ewes to view it as a paranormal phenomenon whose effects destabilize families while making the individual dysfunctional in society.

We recognized that the ill-effects of excessive and sometimes addictive alcohol intake cannot be underrated. This is because alcohol does not only pose a great risk to one's physical well-being, but also destroys one's professional image, credibility, ruins relationships with God and other people, and dampens faith in oneself while filling one's life with despair, distress and desolation. This greatly affects the functionality of the family to which one belongs.

---

[378] www.alcoholics.com.

[379] Lucy D. Ozarin, "Introductory Remarks" in *The Role of the Clergy in Understanding and Counselling the Alcoholic and the Family*. Fargo, North Dakota: North Dakota Agricultural College, 1960 p. 7.

The family flounders as it attempts to adjust to its member who has and is least responsible when responsibility is called for, who is unbearably irritable and egocentric, who embarrasses them in front of friends and spoils their holidays by binges, who spends money on alcohol or drugs that they need for food, and who seems completely oblivious to their welfare or their pleadings.[380]

Here, there is a general picture of interpersonal tragedy as the family is confronted with an individual's alcoholic behaviour. It has been noted that many lives have been lost due to unchecked alcoholism and many families have been shattered for the same reason. Thus, issues of alcoholism in the family cannot be underrated but must be considered as a "real disease that poses danger to real people in the real world."[381] Any meaningful therapeutic process must therefore be "wholistic" and integrative of the family.

From the foregoing, one can conclude that there is probably no problem so far reaching in scope, so devastating in nature and so costly in its effects on the society as alcoholism. Yet, due to its commonality and its prevalent use in rituals in society, its destructive and debilitating effects on the family, and for that matter the larger society, are often overlooked and little is done to alleviate its tragic effects. I have consequently attempted to explore the nature, causes and scope of alcoholism in the family whilst considering the importance of seeking wholeness for family members as well as its implications for the African Christian Church and for pastoral care and counselling. This is to help gain a better understanding or insight into this complex problem while considering the role of the pastoral counsellor and the church in ministering to the alcoholic and the family.

Alcoholism is a family problem. Families are involved with alcoholism as it engulfs them in an ensnaring nightmare. This study, in exploring the quest for wholeness in this context, sought to suggest a new paradigm, one for restoring the alcoholic to wholeness, and affirming spirituality as a potent restoration process. It also emphasizes that such restoration cannot be

---

[380] Clinebell, *Understanding and Counselling,* p. 399f.
[381] www.alcoholics.com, c. 2007.

"wholistic" or complete if it is employed within the context of anxious systems. However, emphasizing spirituality is not to reject the other aspects that make healing whole. Thus, if there should be a "wholistic" recovery, the physical, psychological, social as well as the spiritual healing must be emphasized. This new paradigm which is basically an integrative approach, also calls for an indigenization of family systems theory for any meaningful healing to occur. This is because the family is just as sick as the individual alcoholic. It also seeks to employ indigenous worldview and its usefulness in such a restoration process. It is my contention that when such an approach is employed, it is only then that the theological conceptions of faith, hope and love can be fully realized in restoring the created freedom of the entire family and not only the individual in isolation as they surrender to the sufficiency of the grace of God.

Thus, for any meaningful recovery to take place in restoring the individual into a state of "humanness" or wholeness (*shalom*) the family, whose members are equally sick, must be considered for healing as well. Healing in its entirety which emphasizes totality in relationships intrapersonally, interpersonally and transpersonally, and seeks unity and solidarity, harmonious community, expression of mutual confidence and responsibility, participation in community and fulfilling of one's roles and responsibilities, is what we seek to propose from this study. It is within such a context of meaningful relations and communality that the alcoholic will be able to accentuate his/her self-worth and well-being. Thus, family members and codependants— who are also caught up in this deadly pestilence pattern cannot be left out of this process aimed at fostering growth.

It has been noted above that the system of thought and practice of the Ewes of southeastern Ghana is based on a spiritual ontology and a practical viewpoint that accentuates relationality and communality within the framework of the sacred. Healing as well as counselling in this context is focused on relationships existing between persons and groups whose essential value and worth is to be found in the system of familial, spiritual and intergenerational links within which they are entrenched.[382] To

---

[382] See Lartey, *Pastoral Theology in an Intercultural World.*

this end, a communal sense of life emphasizing relationality and a keen sense of belonging is generally upheld. This opposes an individualistic view which emphasizes aloneness which is very much reflective of western thought and patterns of living. Healing and restoration in this context is therefore focused on restoration of harmonious relationships between humans and throughout the cosmos. Thus, social analysis, family therapy and spiritual recovery are emphasized. This therefore calls for the use of family system therapy and supported by shame theory which calls for a focus on the system rather than the individual, and also restoration of interpersonal relations in any meaningful therapeutic process.

Generally, life in this milieu emphasizes both the sacred and secular. Religion and views of the sacred are transcendent and are very much invasive and pliant in this milieu. These are expressed most clearly in rituals which are aimed at fostering and enhancing harmonious relations between humans and with the unseen world of ancestors, gods and other malevolent spirit entities. Thus, a holistic view of life prevails and this is reflected in the everyday life and activity of the people. For the Ewes, religion is the very life of the people and illnesses are considered not only in the natural sense, but also mystical or supernatural connotations are always sought. Consequently, for the well-being of humans to thrive, there need to be harmony throughout the cosmos. The different aspects of humankind, the social and spiritual life, which interconnect and intertwine must cohere or amalgamate in a meaningful way. This is because in this milieu God is seen as qualitatively present in the sacred as in the secular order. Both the sacred and the secular are seen to cohere strongly without confusion or contradiction.[383] It is these views that influence the Ewe perception of alcoholism as a spiritual disease since the addict loses the aspects of life that makes one functional in relation to others and with God. Consequently, treatment for the alcoholic and his/her family must take into consideration this spiritual worldview.

It was frequently emphasized by the respondents that the alcoholic is one who has lost his/her state of "humanness." In

---

[383] Lartey, *Pastoral Theology in an Intercultural World*, p. 64.

other words, he/she has become something less than a human being. It was, however, interesting to note that in their use of this phrase, the Ewes do not seek to "dehumanize" the alcoholic but rather to suggest that one has become something other than he/she was created to be; one who has lost one's freedom and is now physically, psychologically, socially and spiritually deprived of one's human capacities and can therefore not function as a "normal human being" because one is sick in all of his/her human capacities. Thus, for one to be restored into a state of "humanness" would be a restoration to a state of "wholeness."

Significantly, therefore, healing and restoration in this worldview must seek to reflect "wholism" by considering all the aspects of what makes one "human." Though this study seeks to place more emphasis on the social and spiritual connotations of this illness due to its importance in the worldview of the Ewes, one cannot give singular attention to one aspect of the illness and ignore the others as one seeks to emphasize "wholism" in relation to the recovery of alcoholics. It must therefore be a combination of the physical, psychological, social and spiritual; a combination of all that makes us human.

The *physical* is important because thousands of alcoholics and drug addicts die every year as a result of not only what the toxic substance does to the body, but because if they are not able to secure their drug of choice, they often die in withdrawal. Thus, through an appropriate detoxifying process, appropriately monitored by a physician, efforts must be made to ensure that the alcoholic would "survive," that is, physically remain alive. It has been noted that the most critical organ of the human body affected is the human brain. With the irreparable damage done to the brain by alcohol and other drugs, one needs to pay attention to the ramifications of what it means to come off these drugs and monitor the physical health of people. I suppose this is what the traditional healers seek to use herbalism to achieve. It is therefore very necessary to have treatment centres where people can be monitored with regard to withdrawal symptoms so as to prevent alcoholic convulsions and eventual death. Once this is done meaningfully, the concomitant psychological craving that remains even when a person is sober is eventually eroded.

The *psychological* aspect likewise needs to be addressed

because the illness stymies the emotional growth of people. The emotional growth stops at the point where the person enters into addictive drinking. For example, one who started drinking heavily at the age of fifteen has his/her emotional growth arrested at that age. It therefore takes time to "catch up" emotionally. Hence, it is important to address the psychological characteristics of alcoholics for any meaningful recovery process. Issues of low self-esteem, isolation, selfishness, and rebellion, have to be dealt with in a very meaningful way through an affirmation of one's worth and dignity as a person created in the image of God, and reliance on the sufficiency of God's grace as a source of empowerment or aid in overcoming one's weaknesses.

The *social* dimension which has likewise been continuously emphasized in this book, refers to the impact that the illness has on significant others. It has been noted that family members and significant others become as sick as the addict and need healing as much as the alcohol addict. It is, however, noted that most of these codependents or significant others who are equally affected are never in recovery. These people, spouses, children, partners, and extended family, have their special needs and these must be met through an appropriate recovery process that aims at re-building and restoring mutual love in relationships as well as restoring the dignity and family worth.

It is also very necessary for the alcoholic to be re-socialized because his/her social matrix was for the most part made up of other addicts who were not in recovery. Significantly therefore, it is very necessary for recovering addicts to find an *abstinent peer group* with which to identify. It is for this reason that Alcoholics Anonymous (AA) has been identified as the best "community" for them. Thus, the formation of AA and other 12-step groups in this regard, is very expedient so as to foster their abstemiousness in recovery. Such 12-step programmes are needed not only for the afflicted addict but for the significant others who are adversely affected and have become codependents. This is to help those who are growing (or have grown in an alcoholic environment and whose personalities and outlook on life have been affected by growing up in such an environment) to be able to deal constructively with the stresses and traumas of being codependent. This is very important for the illness not to perpetuate itself in the family and for generations to come.

The *spiritual* focus is what completes the "wholistic" aspect of this illness. It has been suggested that it is the "first" aspect of life that the addict loses and it is the "last" to be restored and I think there is some truth in that statement. Alcoholics Anonymous regards alcoholism as a "spiritual malady." This has been clearly elucidated and affirmed by this study as I noted that "spirituality" means so many different things to so many different people in various cultural contexts. As has been pointed out, it is really difficult to get a definitive "definition" because in some ways, the way the word is understood is contingent upon the culture in which a person lives, as well as the individual experiences that people have that they term as "spiritual" in nature. In this context, however, spirituality is not about spiritual disciplines but about relationships; humans in relationship with the Divine, the environment and with others. In any meaningful restoration process, however, this aspect of the addict that is destroyed is of enormous value and must be considered. It is for this reason as well as the social dimension, that family systems theory is also relevant in bringing healing and total restoration to the family of which the individual is a part through advancement of harmonious relationships.

Considering the spiritual worldview of the Ewes of southeastern Ghana, one cannot help but affirm it as a very potent means of restoring the alcoholic to wholeness. This worldview reflects on the goodness of God in everyday life and experiences. Though sources of affliction of illnesses and diseases are linked to disruption in relations between humans and with the divine, this does not suggest a God who vents evil on His people, but rather suggests a worldview that links evil to human actions and also to malevolent spirit entities. Thus, redirection of alcoholics and their families towards reliance on *"Mawu Segbolisa,"* the great one, who surpasses all, is very necessary for any meaningful recovery. The act of surrender through admission of one's powerlessness over alcohol and turning over of oneself to God is essential in this regard. As with other illnesses, restoration of broken relationships through the reestablishment of harmonious relations between humans and others, and with the cosmos is what is affirmed through this act of surrender. It is only by this that one will be able to humbly affirm one's created freedom in life.

Alcohol addiction is characterized as a *lifestyle disorder*. Using this term is to suggest that it is a disorder of all of the four aforementioned areas of life. Due to the loss of "life" in all these areas that make one "human," there have to be substantive changes in all the four areas noted above if *recovery* is to occur "wholistically." It is worth affirming that human beings resist change. Even though we may know that something is not good for us or even killing us, once we are addicted to it, it is very difficult to give it up. The power of addiction is such that some alcoholics are afraid of what life would be like without alcohol, even when they knew that their drinking was killing them.

A broader theological reflection on the phenomenon of alcoholic dependence and addiction causes us at this point to consider Professor Cook's[384] consideration of two Christian texts for detailed study, on the basis that they appear to reflect a phenomenologically similar experience to that of the subjective compulsion of alcohol dependence. The first of these is St Paul's discussion of the divided self in Romans 7, and the second is in Book 8 of the Confessions of St Augustine of Hippo. Both texts reflect an understanding of the ways in which individuals can struggle within themselves in respect of behaviour to which they aspire. In Romans 7: 15-19, for example, St Paul writes:

> I do not understand my own actions. For I do not do what I want, but I do the very thing I hate. Now if I do what I do not want, I agree that the law is good. But in fact it is no longer I that do it, but sin that dwells within me. For I know that nothing good dwells within me, that is, in my flesh. I can will what is right, but I cannot do it. For I do not do the good I want, but the evil I do not want is what I do.

And now to compare this with the experience of an alcohol dependent woman, married to an alcohol dependent husband, whose story was included in the "Big Book" of Alcoholics Anonymous:

---

[384] Christopher Cook, "A Theology of the Use and Misuse of Alcohol." www.ias.com.

George tried many times to go on the wagon. If I had been sincere in what I thought I wanted more than anything else in life — a sober husband and a happy, contented home — I would have gone on the wagon with him. I did try, for a day or two, but something always would come up that would throw me. It would be a little thing; the rugs being crooked, or any silly little thing that I'd think was wrong, and off I'd go, drinking . . . I reached a stage where I couldn't go into my apartment without a drink. It didn't bother me anymore whether George was drinking or not. I had to have liquor. Sometimes I would lie on the bathroom floor, deathly sick, praying I would die, and praying to God as I always had prayed to Him when I was drinking: "Dear God, get me out of this one and I'll never do it again." And then I'd say, "God, don't pay any attention to me. You know I'll do it tomorrow, the very same thing."[385]

And also with the alcoholic who was interviewed in this study:

. . . all of a sudden I just got into this situation and I still can't understand. Sometimes I seem to be well but at other times I feel so restless. I have had some physical afflictions that set me thinking a lot and it's stressful . . . But it's not my fault. I don't want to drink but it looks like some forces are driving me to.

These kinds of experiences are not alien to humankind. It may not be quite as dramatic, and the implications might not be quite as serious, but we all find ourselves doing things that we know we shouldn't do and then regretting it. We struggle to stop destructive patterns of behaviour and find ourselves doing the very things that we have decided in our minds we will not do. Looked at in this way, it might be argued that alcoholics have a subjective compulsion to do things that they don't want to do. Perhaps it is even a characteristically human experience to have such internal struggles and to be aware of having them. This certainly is not unique to the experience of the addict or alcoholic.

For St Paul, the solution was clear: "*Wretched man that I*

---

[385] Alcoholics Anonymous, *The Big Book*, pp 324-325.

am! Who will rescue me from this body of death? Thanks be to God through Jesus Christ our Lord!"[386] I believe such a state of "wretchedness" is what the Ewes seek to suggest when they argue that one has lost one's state of "humanness" by becoming something other than what he/she was created to be. Turning over oneself unto *"Mawu"* as well as restoring of broken relationships in all dimensions now becomes the key to wholeness.

For St. Paul, the grace of God in Jesus, the Christ, is the only way to become free from this struggle. Augustine of Hippo in a similar vein emphasizes the necessity of this grace to set us free from the struggle set up by the division of the human will against itself. Though post-modern culture is much less happy to accept the particularity of this solution, Alcoholics Anonymous adopted a similar, albeit not so Christocentric, understanding in the second of its 12 Steps: *We came to believe that Power greater than ourselves could restore us to sanity.* The necessity of such a "Higher Power," whatever it might be, as a component of a spiritual recovery from alcoholism was to become fundamental to the philosophy of Alcoholics Anonymous. This is also affirmed by the worldview of the Ewes with the emphasis on the reviving of relationships between humans and the Divine, who has ultimate power and control over all of creation, including humans. For St Paul and St Augustine, however, faith in Christ was the only pathway to freedom from the divided self. This suggests that grace is an important component of recovery and to separate it from any healing model will highly impoverish such an approach. It is therefore very necessary to redirect addicts to this loving God because *Mawunyo,* God is good.

The ultimate goal of the Christian gospel is wholeness; the restoration of fallen humanity and the redirection of men and women to the image of God. One must therefore seek communion with a higher power, the ultimate, God, so as to be able to confront oneself, acknowledge one's weakness or powerlessness, and consequently move toward attaining wholeness. This is what Lartey and Masamba ma Mpolo sought to assert when they wrote about wholeness through meaningful

---

[386] Romans 7: 24-25.

restoration of relations intrapersonally, interpersonally and transpersonally in the African milieu. Doing this meaningfully involves total surrender on the part of those afflicted and the many others affected, and also ultimately humbling oneself in this process as one relies on God's grace to strengthen him/her to overcome one's powerlessness.

According to Luther, God's grace is a priceless and soothing medicine. He suggests that reliance on oneself wearies the soul and brings on physical maladies but "the grace of God helps people in all their afflictions — body, mind, and spirit."[387] This is, however, emphasized within the context of one's relationships, to God and to other people. It is invariably the definitive focal point of spirituality which ultimately propels the alcoholic and the affected family toward attaining wholeness. One can therefore not deliver oneself from the power of alcohol but through reliance on the grace and power of God within the context of loving relations. The family is therefore an important reality within whose context wholeness can be sustained. In effect, as long as the Ghanaian Ewe family continues to reflect their spirituality within the context of the family, and as long as their fundamental view of life is one of relationality and communality under the overshadowing guidance of a loving God, healing for the family is very paramount in bringing total restoration for the alcoholic in all of his/her dimensions of life.

To return to the broader issue of total restoration of the alcoholic and his/her family, a "wholistic" approach that seeks to emphasize the social and spiritual dimensions, but not neglecting the physical and psychological, is what is being emphasized. It is to an end of this "wholistic" recovery process that the place of the pastoral counsellor is very significant in redirecting individual alcoholics and their families *from* the power of alcohol *to* the power of God.

It is very well noted that people turn to clergypersons for assistance with their problems far more than anyone else in the community. The clergy are the frontline of defence in relation to caregivers in helping people meet their problems in living.

---

[387] Steinke, *Healthy Congregations*, p. 82f.

This puts the clergyperson in a unique position in relation to those who can be easily approached for help and to be seen by those who have problems with living. Though attitudes toward drinking vary to several degrees, the pastoral counsellor must view alcoholism as a family problem and helping both the alcoholic and the family regain their dignity, respect and acceptance is therefore paramount. In other words, through meaningful therapeutic relationships, faith, hope, and worth of the alcoholic is restored within the context of mutual restoration of faith, hope and love for the family as well.

Traditionally, total healing comes through an act of divination where the source of the problem is sought and the alcoholic delivered from the gods through acts of pacification, sacrifice or purification, coupled with restoring of harmony between one human being and the other. According to Berinyuu, the pastoral counsellor thus plays the role of the diviner helping the client to be able to answer the question, why? The counsellor, in playing this role, thus seeks to help the addict and his/her family to find meaning in life and answers to such existential questions that they might have. This can be done through performing of pastoral functions such as prayer and rituals, as well as through reframing of assumptions. Pastoral counsellors must therefore endeavour to explore and understand these concepts within the context of the people so as to be able to employ its therapeutic power.

In fostering family cohesion through meaningful communication and de-triangulation so as to facilitate restoration to wholeness and consequently growth, the use of metaphors, images and stories that inform is very helpful as it seeks to breed a desire to change. This calls for a good understanding of family systems theory in dealing with alcoholism in this regard. It has been suggested that implicit in all pastoral work is the awareness that the minister is influenced by issues relating to his/her own family of origin. The pastoral counsellor must therefore be well differentiated or must be able to maintain his/her own emotional equilibrium so as to be able to offer meaningful help without projecting one's own unresolved issues.

I have suggested earlier that the philosophy and ideals of any society informs and influences its people in identifying problems and forms of therapy. Any diagnostic process towards healing or wholeness must therefore consider this worldview. This awareness is necessary for pastoral counselling with the alcoholic and his/her family in this milieu as well. For there to be any meaningful effort at providing pastoral care in this context, any process must be contextual and action-reflection oriented. It should be rooted in the contextual worldview of the people as well as based on biblical and theological truths. It is in the light of this that this study calls for indigenization of family systems theory since it clearly reflects the communal and relational worldview of the people.

Among the Ewes, religion is the very life of the people. Thus, sustaining life is tantamount to upholding religious ideals and beliefs. For this reason, I contend that healing and wholeness in this context can be total when it seeks to find peace with God, and with others. Living spiritually within this context is living in harmony in relationships. This suggests that though spirituality is of primary importance, it cannot be meaningful outside the context of the family or without considering the general stresses and traumas of the affected family.

Addiction has a life of its own and the alcoholic has therefore set in motion powerful forces over which he/she has no control. Although alcoholics can live spiritually, as suggested earlier, they are in constant conflict because alcohol demands to be a replacement for God. God is displaced as the centre of life and alcohol thus becomes the "saving grace."[388] When alcoholics are able to replace their alcoholic sense with a healthy sense and reflect on the immediate and long-term negative consequences of drinking, they are more likely to maintain and foster sobriety and less apt to drink. This, the pastoral counsellor must seek to affirm not only for the healing of the alcoholic, but in restoring the whole family to wholeness.

Denial has been noted as a fundamental obstruction to the treatment of alcoholism. Once the problem is not acknowledged and accepted, one rejects all forms of treatment aimed at correcting that affliction that has engulfed the whole family. It has been suggested that denial is influenced by shame and

---

[388] Kraft, p. 95.

disgrace which invariably entangles the whole family in a systemic conspiracy of silence. Shame is influenced by a feeling of worthlessness and the fear of exposure which is fostered by the severing of the interpersonal bridge. This is to suggest that the antidote for shame is acceptance.[389] The pastoral counsellor or therapist must therefore be involved in restoring the interpersonal as well as intrapersonal bridge so as to be able to eschew that fear and foster wholeness. Due to the patriarchal nature of this worldview, the pastoral counsellor who is held in high regard in this society is in a unique position to assume the function of doing intervention with family members so that they are not "taken down" with the alcoholic and his/her disease. Also through meaningful education, people in general and the church in particular, must be educated on the realities of alcohol addiction so as to help alter their attitudes generally towards alcohol, alcoholism and the alcoholic so as to make ministry in this regard effective.

Also, I have sought to suggest that love and ultimate concern is paramount in any therapeutic process for the alcoholic and his/her family. Pastoral counsellors, as well as other caregivers must meaningfully show empathy, warmth and understanding, and must also be non-judgmental in their approach to dealing with all those involved with this problem. This unconditional, non-judgmental process is the deepest point of love as reflected in one's freedom in Christ. This is also very essential for the "social support groups" which I have sought to propose earlier for the re-socialization process for the addict as well as codependents that are equally affected.

Since families may be contending with their own denial, anxieties, and shame, the church must make a strenuous effort to emphasize for recovering people to come to the knowledge of the meaning of Divine providence; to the knowledge of the presence of a Reality that is more than oneself, beyond the self and greater than oneself; and who has all-capacity and power to provide for the alcoholic. According to Dr. Livingstone Buama, "A relevant church is considered as a harbinger of faith, hope and love." For him, when one loses hope, one is reduced

---

[389] Albers, *Shame and the Conspiracy of Silence*, p. 62f

to something less than human.[390] The church must therefore not use the Bible as a tool of chastisement of the alcoholic, but rather through meaningful education, assume its position as a facilitator of this spiritual, total and complete encounter with God through healing and holistic transcendental reflections. The church can therefore be a helpful organization in assisting the alcoholic and his/her family in dealing with problems related to alcoholism. The church can do this by offering acceptance through warmth and empathetic understanding of the alcoholic and his/her family rather than being judgmental. Also, through its family and individual counselling, the church can prevent its occurrence.

This contention is not just a spiritual wishful-fulfillment or a kind of double talk, but must be acknowledged as a clinical and effective phenomenon that facilitates recovery and wholeness for the alcoholic and his/her family. These assertions are not only relevant for pastoral counsellors and the church, but must be seen as relevant for other caregivers, psychologists, psychiatrists, treatment facilities, as well as the general public. An understanding of the effects on the family or how families are involved with alcoholism is also very helpful in providing care and ultimate restoration. It must be understood that in emphasizing healing for the family, this does not take the focus off the individual, but rather an attempt to seek restoration of the entire family system network in its totality.

It is worth emphasizing that this work is not exhaustive, but it is hoped that it will begin a process of gaining a better understanding of this all-pervasive, encompassing and insidious problem of alcoholism in the African milieu and its implications for the Christian church. Also, though the commonality of alcohol as a social and ritual drink in this regard is suggested to be a great factor contributing to its abuse; certainly, other factors such as advertisements are currently viewed as having more influence over the youth. It will therefore be very necessary for further research to be done in this area to explore its effect, so that the life of future generations would not to be jeopardized.

---

[390] Livingstone Buama. An Address delivered at the Alumni Congress of Trinity Theological Seminary on 14 March, 2007.

Bibliography

Akyeampong, E. *Drink, Power, and Cultural Change: A Social History of Alcohol in Ghana, c. 1800 to Recent Time.* Portsmouth, NH. 1996.

Albers, Robert. "The Challenge of the Future." *Journal of Ministry in Addiction and Recovery,* Vol. 1 (2) The Haworth Press, 1994 1-8.

———*Shame: A Faith Perspective.* New York, The Haworth Press, 1995.

———"Continuity and Change in the Continuum of Care." *Journal of Ministry in Addiction and Recovery,* Vol. 5 (2) The Haworth Press, (1998): 1-12.

———"The Search for Meaning." *Journal of Ministry in Addiction and Recovery,* Vol. 6 (2) 1999. 1-9.

———"Shame and the Conspiracy of Silence." *Journal of Ministry in Addiction and Recovery,* Vol. 7 (1) 2000: 51-68.

———"The Spirit and Spirituality of Twelve Step Groups" *Journal of Ministry in Addiction and Recovery,* Vol. 6(1) 1999: 1-8.

———"Spiritual Barriers to Recovery." *Journal of Ministry in Addiction and Recovery.* Vol. 5 (1) 1998: 1-11.

——— "Spirituality and Religion: Allies or Adversaries?" *Journal of Ministry in Addiction and Recovery,* Vol. 4 (2) 1997: 1-8.

———"Transformation: The Key to Recovery." *Journal of Ministry in Addiction and Recovery,* Vol. 4 (1) 1997: 21-36.

Alcoholics Anonymous. *The Story of How Many Thousands of Men and Women Have Recovered from Alcoholism.* New York: Alcoholics Anonymous World Services, Inc. 1976.

Apthorp, Stephen P. *Alcohol and Substance Abuse: A Clergy Handbook.* Wilton, Connecticut: Morehouse-Barlow Co., Inc., 1985.

Asamoah-Gyadu, Kwabena J. *African Charismatics: Current Developments Within Independent Indigenous Pentecostalism in Ghana.* African Christian Press Edition. Leiden, The Netherlands: Koninklijke Brill NV, 2005.

Asquith, Glen, Jr. "Empirical Theology: Boisen as Pastoral Theologian." *The Journal of Pastoral Care* 7 (2) 1980 7f.

———"The Case Study Method of Anton T. Boisen." *The Journal of Pastoral Care* 34, 1980 84-94.

———*Awakening: A Substance Abuse Therapeutic Program.* Treatment Manual, August 1992.

Baeta, Christian, G. *Christianity and Healing,* ORITA: Ibadan, 1967.

Berinyuu, A.A. *Pastoral Care to the Sick in Africa: An Approach to Transcultural Pastoral Theology.* Frankfurt: Peter Lang, 1988.

Bratter Thomas E. and Gary G. Forrest. *Alcoholism and Substance Abuse: Strategies for Clinical Intervention.* New York: The Free Press,1985.

Bohler, Carolyn J. "Essential Elements of Family Systems Approaches to Pastoral Care and Counselling." In *Clinical Handbook of Pastoral Care and Counselling.* Volume 1. Expanded Edition. Ed. Robert Wicks, Richard Parsons and Donal Capps. Mahwah, NJ: Paulist Press, 1993.

Boisen, A.T. *The Exploration of the Inner World.* New York: Harper, 1936.

———*Out of Depths: An Autobiographical Study of Mental Disorder and Religious*

Experience. New York: Harper & Brothers, 1960.

Bowen, Murray. *Family Therapy in Clinical Practice.* Northvale, New Jersey: Jason Aronson Inc., 1978.

Campbell, Ted A. *Methodist Doctrine: The Essentials.* Nashville: Abingdon Press, 1999.

Carr, Anne. "On Feminist Theology." In *Spirituality. Ministry and Field Education. Key Resources:* Volume V. Ed. Beisswenger Donald, Doran McCarty and Lynn Rhodes. Nashville and San Francisco: The Association for Theological field Education, 1986.

Carr, Wesley *et. al.* eds. *The New Dictionary of Pastoral Studies.* Grand Rapids, Michigan: W.B. Eerdmans Publishing Co., 2002.

Carroll, Charles R. *Drugs in Modern Science.* Dubuque, Iowa: Wm. C. Brown Publishers, 1985.

Corey, Gerald. *Theory and Practice of Counselling and Psychotherapy,* Fifth Edition. Pacific Grove, California: Brooks /Cole Publishing Company, 1996.

Couture, Pamela D. & Rodney Hunter, eds. *Pastoral Care and Spiritual Conflict.* Nashville: Abingdon Press, 1995.

Clinebell, Howard. *Understanding and Counselling Persons with Alcohol, Drug, and Behavioural Addictions: Counselling for Recovery and Prevention Using Psychology and Religion.* Revised and Enlarged edition. Nashville: Abingdon Press, 1998.

Dejong Alexander and Martin Doot. *Dying for a Drink: A Pastor and a Physician Talk about Alcoholism.* Grand Rapids, Michigan: William B. Eerdmans Publishing Company, 1999.

Dickson, Kwesi. *Theology in Africa Today.* London: Longman & Todd, Orbis Books, 1984.

Douglas, Mary ed. *Constructive Drinking Perspectives on Drink from Anthropology.* Cambridge, 1987.

Eugene, Chester J. ed. *The Role of the Clergy in Understanding and Counselling the Alcoholic and the Family.* Fargo, North Dakota: North Dakota Agricultural College, 1960.

Friedman, Edwin H. *Generation to Generation: Family Process in Church and Synagogue.* New York: The Guilford Press, 1985.

Fiawoo, Kwasi F. *Toko Atolia.* London: Longman, Green, and Co. Ltd., 1962.

Gaba, Christian R. "The Religious Life of the People." In *A Handbook of Eweland. Volume 1: The Ewes of Southeastern Ghana,* ed. Agbodeka Francis. Accra: Woeli Publishing Services, 1997.

Gadamer, Hans-George. *Truth and Method.* New York: Seabury Press, 1975.

Gavua, Kodzo. "Religious Practices." In *A Handbook of Eweland. Vol II: The Northern Ewes in Ghana.* Woeli Publishing Services, 2000.

Gerkin, Charles. *The Living Human Document: Revisioning Pastoral Counselling in a Hermeneutical Mode.* Nashville: Abingdon Press, 1984.

Gerkins, Charles. *Widening the Horizons: Pastoral Responses to a Fragmented Society.* Philadelphia: Westminster Press, 1986.

Ghunney, Joseph K. *Peer Counselling Manual: Life Skills for Young People.* New York: General Board of Global Ministries-United Methodist Church, 2005.

———*African Spiritual Worldview: Its Impact on Alcohol and Other Drug Use by Senior Secondary School Students in Ghana.* A PhD Dissertation. Maryland, Loyola College: April, 1994.

Gyekye, Kwame. *African Cultural Values: An Introduction.* Accra, Ghana: Sankofa Publishing Company, 2003.

———*An Essay on African Philosophical Thought: The Akan Conceptual Scheme,* Revised Edition. Philadelphia: Temple University Press, 1995.

Hansen, Philip L. *Alcoholism: The Tragedy of Abundance.* Minneapolis: Park Printing Service, 1982.

Holt, Bradley. *Thirsty for God.* Minneapolis: Augsburg Press, 1993.

Horton, Donald. "The Functions of Alcohol in Primitive Societies: A Cross-Cultural Study," *Quarterly Journal of Studies on Alcohol* 4 (2) 1943. pp. 199-320.

Hunsinger, Deborah Van Deusen. *Theology and Pastoral Counselling: A New Interdisciplinary Approach.* Grand Rapids, Michigan: William Erdman's Publishing Co., 1995.

Idowu, E.B. *African Traditional Religion.* London: SCM Press, 1973.

Igenoza, Andrew Olu. "Wholeness in African Experience, Christian Perspectives." In *The Church and Healing: Echoes from Africa,* ed. Lartey Emmanuel, Daisy Nwachuku & Kasonga we Kasonga. Frankfurt: Peter Lang, 1994.

Jarvis, Tracey J, Jenny Tebbutt and Richard Mattick. *Treatment Approaches for Alcohol and Drug Dependence: An Introductory Guide.* England: John Wiley and Sons Ltd.

Jellinek, E.M. *The Disease Concept of Alcoholism.* New Haven: Hillhouse Press, 1960.

Kaufman, Edward. "Family Therapy in the Treatment of Alcoholism." In *Alcoholism and Substance Abuse: Strategies for Clinical Intervention,* ed. Bratter Thomas E. & Gary G. Forrest. New York: The Free Press, 1985.

Kaufman, Gershen. *Shame: The Power of Caring.* 3rd edition. Rochester, Vermont: Schenkman Books Inc., 1992.

Keller, John E. *Ministering to Alcoholics.* Revised Edition. Minneapolis: Augsburg Fortress, 1991.

Kilson, Marion. "Libation in Ga Ritual," *Journal of Religion in Africa* 2 (3) 1969 161-178.

Kraft, William F. *The Normal Alcoholic.* New York: Alba House, 1999.

Kramer, Jeannette R. *Family Interfaces: Transgenerational Patterns.* New York: Brunner/Mazel, 1985.

Lartey, Emmanuel Y.(ed) *The Church and Healing: Echoes from Africa.* African Pastoral Series; vol 2, Frankfurt Main, 1994.

———*Pastoral Counselling in Inter-Cultural Perspective,* Frankfurt, Peter Lang, 1987.

———*Pastoral Theology in an Intercultural World.* Epworth Press, 2006.

———"Some Contextual Implications for Pastoral Counselling in Ghana." In *Pastoral Care and Counselling in Africa Today,* Jean Masamba ma Mpolo and Daisy Nwachuku, Eds. Frankfurt am Main: Peter Lang, 1991.

Lennon, Eric and David Lee. *Breaking Glass: Finding Freedom from Alcoholism.* U.K: Marshall Pickering, 1987.

Love, Mary A. *Potpourri for Christian Educators*. Revised edition. Charlotte, N.C.: A.M.E. Zion Publishing House, 1988.

Ma Mpolo, Masamba. *Perspectives on African Pastoral Counselling*. Ministerial Formation: Programme on Theological Education. Geneva, 1984.

——"Spirituality and Counselling for Healing and Liberation: The Context and Praxis of African Pastoral activity and Psychotherapy." In *The Church and Healing: Echoes from Africa*, ed. Lartey Emmanuel, Daisy Nwachuku, and Kasonga Wa Kasonga. Frankfurt: Peter Lang, 1994.

Mandelbaum, D.G. "Alcohol and Culture." *Current Anthropology* 6 1965: 281-293.

Mbiti, John S. *African Religions and Philosophy*. Second, Revised and Enlarged Edition. London: Heinemann [1969] 1990.

McClendon, James. *Biography as Theology: How Life Stories Can Remake Today's Theology Primary*. Nashville: Abingdon Press, 1974.

Meyer, Birgit. *Translating the Devil: Religion and Modernity Among the Ewe in Ghana*. Trenton, NJ: Africa World Press Inc., 1999.

Nelson-Adzakpey, Ted. *Penance and Expiatory Sacrifice among the Ghanaian-Ewe and their Relevance to the Christian Religion*. Rome: Tipografia Olimpica, 1982.

Nelson, Ellis C. Ed. *Issues Facing Christian Educators Today: A Report Based on The World Institute on Christian Education Meeting in Nairobi, Kenya*. World Council on Christian Education: July 1967.

Nichols, Michael P. *Family Therapy: Concepts and Methods*. Needham Heights, MA: Allyn and Bacon, 1984.

Nukunya, G. K. "Festivals." In *A Handbook of Eweland*. Volume 1: The Ewes of Southeastern Ghana, ed. Francis Agbodeka. Accra: Woeli Publishing Services, 1997.

——*Kinship and Marriage Among the Anlo Ewe*. London: University Press, 1969.

——"Social and Political Organizations." In *A Handbook of Eweland. Volume 1: The Ewes of Southeastern Ghana*. Accra: Woeli Publishing Services, 1997.

——*Tradition and Change: The Case of the Family*. Accra: Ghana Universities Press, 1992.

——*Tradition and Change in Ghana: An Introduction to Sociology*. Second Edition. Accra: Ghana Universities Press, 2003.

Opoku, Kofi Asare. *West African Traditional Religion*. Nigeria: FEP International Private Limited, 1978.

Parrinder, Geoffrey. *West African Religion*. London: The Epworth Press, 1961.

Pattison, Stephen. *SHAME: Theory, Therapy, Theology*. Cambridge, U.K.: Cambridge University Press, 2000.

Presbyterian Church. *Alcohol Use and Abuse: The Social and Health Effects. Reports and Recommendations by the Presbyterian Church (USA)* Louisville, KY: Office of Health Ministries.

Rattray, R.S. *Ashanti*. Oxford: Clarendon Press, 1923.

Room, Robin "Alcohol Problems and the City," *British Journal of Addiction* 85 (1990). pp. 1395-1402.

Saliger, Robert V. *How to Help an Alcoholic: A Brief Medical Summarization with Pastoral Suggestions and Tests*. Columbus: School and College Service, 1951.

Sarpong, Peter. *Girls Nobility Rites in Ashanti*. Accra: Ghana Publishing Corporation, 1977.

——*Peoples Differ: An Approach to Inculturation in Evangelism*. Accra, Ghana: Sub-Saharan Publishers, 2002.

Schreiter, Robert J. *Constructing Local Theologies*. Maryknoll, NY: Orbis Books, 1985.

Schultz, Stephen J. *Family Systems Thinking*. New Jersey: Jason Aronson Inc., 1984.

Seward, Hiltner, *Preface to Pastoral Theology*. Nashville: Abingdon Press, 1958.

Senah, K. A. "Blofo Tshofa: Local Perception of Medicines in a Ghanaian Rural Community." In *Medicines, Meanings and Context*, ed. Etkin N. and M. Tan., 1991.

Senah, Kodzo. "Traditional and Modern Health Care Practices." In *A Handbook of Eweland. Volume 1: The Ewes of Southeastern Ghana*, ed. Agbodeka Francis. Accra: Woeli Publishing Services, 1997.

Serebo, Boris. "Total Alcohol Consumption as an Index of Anxiety Among Urbanized Africans," *British Journal of Psychiatry* 67 (1972) p. 251-254.

Smedes, Lewis. *Shame and Grace: Healing the Shame We Don't Deserve*. Harper San Francisco: Zondervan Publishing House.

Spangler, John D. *Pastoral Care of Young Drug Users and Their Families*. New York: National Council of Churches, Division of Christian Life and Mission.

Spickard, Anderson and Barbara Thompson. *Dying for a Drink: What You Should Know About Alcoholism*. Dallas: Word Publishing, 1985.

Stanton, Duncan M. "The Family and Drug Abuse: Concepts and Rationale." In *Alcoholism and Substance Abuse: Strategies for Clinical Intervention*, ed. Bratter Thomas E. & Gary G. Forrest. New York: The Free Press, 1985.

Steinke, Peter. *Healthy Congregations: A Systems Approach*. The Alban Institute, 1996.

Stotts, Jack L. *Shalom: The Content of the Peaceable City*. Nashville: Abingdon Press, 1973.

Tiebout, Harry. *The Act of Surrender in a Therapeutic Process*. New York: National Council on Alcohol, n.d.

Twumasi, P.A. *Medical Systems in Ghana*. Accra: Ghana Publishing Corporation, 1975.

Williamson, S. G. *Akan Religion and the Christian Faith: A Comparative Study of the Impact of Two Religions*, ed. Kwesi Dickson. Accra: Ghana Universities Press, 1965.

UNPUBLISHED WORKS

Akrong, Abraham. "African Religions, Media and Health: An Overview." A Paper presented at the World Association for Christian Communication Conference on Religion, Media and Health in West Africa, December 4, 2006.

Asamoah-Gyadu, Kwabena J. "Conquering Satan, Demons, Principalities, and Powers in African Religions: A Ghanaian Perspective on Religion, Evil and Deliverance," n.d. p.1.

Asamoah-Gyadu, Kwabena J. "Rethinking African Worldviews of Mystical Causality." A Paper Presented at the World Association for Christian

Communicators/ Trinity Theological Seminary Conference on Religion, Media and Health in West Africa, 5 December, 2006.

Fayose, Cyril. "Healing Wounds: A Ghanaian Christian Perspective on Intractable Conflict. The Case of the Evangelical Presbyterian Church Ghana." A PhD Thesis. St. Paul, Minnesota: Luther Seminary, 2001.

Ghunney, Joseph K. "African Spiritual Worldview: Its impact on Alcohol and Other Drug Use by Senior Secondary Schools in Ghana." A Ph.D Thesis. Maryland: Loyola College, 1994.